THE EASY GLUTEN-FREE
COOKBOOK

The Easy Gluten-Free

COOKBOOK

FAST AND FUSS-FREE RECIPES FOR BUSY PEOPLE ON A GLUTEN-FREE DIET

Lindsay Garza

ROCKRIDGE PRESS

ADVENTURE AWAITS!
—*Lindsay*

Contents

Introduction

FOR AS LONG AS I CAN REMEMBER, feeling sick every day was just how life was for me. I was so used to it, I didn't realize how much it was limiting my life—the relentless fatigue, the constant brain fog, not to mention always worrying about where the nearest bathroom was. It got even worse when I was a teenager, to the point that I unintentionally lost almost 25 pounds in three months. I felt like I was 18 going on 80. I spent almost nine years going from doctor to doctor, trying to figure out what was wrong, but no one thought to ask about my diet. Then, thankfully, when I was 25, a doctor finally figured out the main culprit: gluten.

Gluten is a protein that naturally occurs in wheat and other grains, and is used in many processed foods. If you, like me, have allergies or an autoimmune disorder that prevents you from processing gluten, eating it can wreak havoc on your body. But once I cleared gluten from my diet, I finally gained my life back.

For the first time, I've had power over what I do and how I feel. I can travel the world, eat out, go to family events, and really experience everything this world has to offer. Granted, all those things have their challenges when you have to be gluten-free, but knowing what you need to avoid and taking specific precautions to keep yourself healthy is well worth the work.

Yes, there are definitely some challenges of eating gluten-free, especially when you're on the go. Having food ready and available is key, but I wouldn't recommend relying on all the prepackaged gluten-free foods and baked goods out there. Just because it's gluten-free doesn't mean it's good for you. Certain products are marketed as health food because they lack gluten, but take a gander at those nutrition labels, my friends, and you'll find that the first ingredient is often sugar! Not to mention they can be outrageously priced. Of course you can treat yourself once in a while, but we most definitely don't need the amount of sugar and fat in those prepackaged products on a daily basis.

Making your own gluten-free food at home gives you total control of what goes into your body. While there may be a few challenges to leading this lifestyle, I'll tell you this: It is totally possible, and you don't have to be a food scientist or an expert chef to do it.

I like to make my life as simple as possible. In my opinion, the less time in the kitchen, the better—that gives you more time to live your life with friends and family. I spend my days creating quick, easy, and delicious gluten-free food, but at heart, I'm a lazy cook. Recipes with massive lists of ingredients and ten pages of instructions are like the plague to me. I prefer to keep it simple, for my sanity and yours.

In this cookbook, you'll find the kinds of recipes I like: easy, simple meals you can make on a hectic weeknight—often with fewer than five ingredients, in under 30 minutes, and/or in a single pot. These are recipes you'll keep coming back to week after week because they're so quick, easy, and delicious, with wholesome, natural ingredients you can feel confident serving to your family. All recipes in this book are gluten-free, and many are also nut-free and dairy-free (or can be made with nondairy substitutes).

Another thing you'll find in this cookbook? Lots of Mexican-inspired flavors! They've always been a favorite of mine, even though I grew up in the Midwest, where the food tends more toward root vegetables and casseroles. My mother and I would make a huge bowl of guacamole and split it perfectly down the middle—one side was hers, the other was mine, and we refused to share with each other or anyone else. Serendipitously, I ended up marrying into a Mexican family, and I discovered that Mexican cuisine isn't just delicious—a lot of it is also naturally gluten-free! My husband has brought many authentic Mexican dishes to our kitchen throughout the years. I've taken them and made them my own, and now I'm sharing some of my favorites with you.

If you love easy, nutritious comfort food that's completely free of gluten, with a dash of Mexican flavor here and there, *The Easy Gluten-Free Cookbook* is for you. All it takes is a little patience and some guidance, and you'll be making delicious gluten-free meals at home—and living the full, healthy life you've always wanted.

CHAPTER ONE

Understanding the Gluten-Free Diet

WHAT THE HECK IS GLUTEN, AND WHERE IS IT FOUND?

Those are the first questions that come to mind when the daunting task of gluten-free eating comes up. Gluten is a protein complex found in grains like wheat, barley, and rye. (Other grains like corn and rice contain different proteins that do not include gluten.) It helps give dough its sticky, elastic quality, and it makes baked goods like bread, pizza, and bagels soft and chewy. Because of those qualities, gluten is often used in products where you wouldn't expect to find wheat, like soups, sauces, and processed meats and cheeses.

Most people can eat gluten with no problem, but for people with celiac disease, gluten intolerance, or gluten allergies, eating a slice of bread can feel like drinking poison. Symptoms range from gastrointestinal discomfort, vomiting, and heartburn to joint pain, migraines, and an overall confusion and lack of focus known as "brain fog."

If you've just learned you can't eat gluten, you probably feel a little overwhelmed. As if giving up bread weren't enough, now you have to figure out if there's gluten in your salad dressing? You'll find, though, that with some education and a bit of time to learn the ropes, you'll be well on your way to eating a gluten-free diet. While you may not believe me now, it becomes easier the more you do it. Soon you'll find yourself preparing meals and even baked goods that no one would guess are gluten-free!

Most important, those tasty meals can clear up your gluten-related symptoms and give you more energy. I found I didn't truly know what being healthy felt like until I cut gluten from my diet. The recipes in this cookbook will help get you on the right track! Let's dive in.

GUIDELINES FOR THE GLUTEN-FREE DIET

This book is all about making your life easier. Here are five simple guidelines that will spare you figurative and literal headaches.

Read your labels. When buying prepackaged food, it's very important to read the nutrition labels and find out everything you can about where a given product comes from and how it was manufactured. Remember, gluten shows up in all kinds of processed foods where you wouldn't necessarily expect it, from soy sauce to potato chips, and even a supposedly gluten-free food can make you sick if it was produced in a factory that also makes wheat products. It's best to buy products made in a dedicated, gluten-free certified plant, but there are times when this simply isn't an option. If a label provides incomplete information, reach out to the company via phone or email. They should be able to tell you more about how a given product is made and whether it could have encountered any possible cross-contaminations during the process.

Stick to the perimeter of the grocery store. You don't have to worry about reading labels if you shop the outer edges of the store, where whole foods like produce, meat, and fish are kept. Fresh vegetables and fruits are naturally gluten-free! Buying plenty of them makes it easier to keep yourself fed (not to mention easier to stay in shape).

Keep it simple. Seek out recipes that involve minimal ingredients and take under 30 minutes to prepare. Taking on complicated recipes right off the bat can be disheartening. Gluten-free cooking—and especially gluten-free baking—

may be different from what you're used to, and you don't want to end up feeling that it's way too hard for you or that you'll never be able to enjoy food again. Keep it simple at first, and then work your way up when you're feeling more confident and adventurous.

Be prepared. When eating out, call ahead or look up the menu in advance to learn about that restaurant's cooking practices. Do their sauces and soups use gluten? Do they prepare gluten-free dishes where they won't be cross-contaminated? Eat at home before you head to a party, just in case they don't have any food you can safely ingest. It may be slightly inconvenient sometimes, but thinking ahead lets you live your life without getting sick or going hungry.

Minimize prepackaged gluten-free products. Many of these products, particularly desserts, use extra sugar and fat to make up for the missing wheat flour. Plus they're expensive! Either make your own version of those foods at home using less sugar, or buy them only occasionally, as a treat. Everything in moderation.

THE COMFORTABLE, CONVENIENT GLUTEN-FREE LIFE

With some guidance, you can make your gluten-free life comfortable, convenient, and easy. It's been over three years since my diagnosis, and here are ten ways I've found to make eating gluten-free easier.

1. **Keep snacks on hand.** I don't just get hungry—I get hangry (hungry + angry). So I recommend always having some sort of gluten-free food on hand to get you through the next couple of hours. There may be times when you can't quickly grab something from a deli the way you used to.

2. **Cook at home.** Cooking at home is the easiest—and healthiest—way to safely eat your meals, especially at the beginning of your gluten-free journey. You have control over the ingredients, and if you've gotten rid of all gluten-containing ingredients in your kitchen, you don't have to worry about cross-contamination as you might at a restaurant.

3. **Make your kitchen gluten-free.** The best way to make sure you don't accidentally ingest gluten is to make your entire household gluten-free. That means spouse, kids, or other family members can eat gluten while they're at work or school, but not at home. In many cases, however, that's

just not possible to enforce, so another option is to designate a section of your kitchen counter as a "gluten-free safe area." You might place a separate cutting board, toaster, or other kitchen items in this safe area so they don't get cross-contaminated with wheat crumbs. Just to be sure, though, always thoroughly wipe down that counter before making yourself food.

4. **Plan out your week.** Every Sunday, I love to plan out what I'm going to eat for the upcoming week, write it down, and then shop for those items. That way, I don't have to stress out about food after a hectic workday, and I'm never caught without something safe to eat. Planning your week and figuring out your meals in advance helps a lot.

5. **Make extra.** Who likes to cook every night? Not me. I often double or even triple certain recipes so my husband and I have plenty of leftovers.

6. **Use your freezer.** Of course, sometimes when you have plenty of leftovers, you get tired of eating the same meal day after day. Freezing those leftovers allows me to reheat a dish weeks later when I'm in the mood for it again (and not in the mood for cooking).

7. **Look for a gluten-free certification seal.** A seal from the Gluten-Free Certification Organization means that group has verified that a given product does not contain gluten and hasn't been cross-contaminated by gluten during the manufacturing process. You'll find that some products say "gluten-free" on the label but don't have the gluten-free certification seal. In that case, I contact the company and ask how its products are manufactured, just to be safe.

8. **Make connections.** There are plenty of gluten-free communities and groups out there, especially on social media. They provide a great place to swap recipes, point out new gluten-free products, and share responses they've received from companies regarding their products. Most important, they connect you with people who have been through what you're going through and can provide moral support. We are stronger together!

9. **Enlist your family.** Support from family and friends can really do wonders. Educate them on what gluten is, where it can be found, and what it does to you if you consume it. If they understand what you're going through, they can support and assist you while you make this change.

10. **Go and live your life!** This one is the most important. Just because you have to avoid gluten does not mean you'll never be able to go places or eat out again. In fact, you'll enjoy your life more once your food is no longer making you sick all the time. Yes, you'll have to make some changes, but living your life as you normally would will make this transition that much easier.

SUPER EASY RECIPES

You get home after working all day, your children are running around the house, and you have only a couple of precious hours before they need to get to bed. Sound familiar? We do not, I repeat, *we do not* have hours upon hours to spend in the kitchen!

The Easy Gluten-Free Cookbook is here to help. You'll find that almost all the recipes in this book fall into one or more of the following categories:

One-Pot or One-Pan recipes: The fewer dishes you have to wash, the better! These recipes can be all made in a single pot or pan. Some also include conversions for those wanting to use a slow cooker or pressure cooker.

Sheet Pan recipes: Much like the one-pot recipes, these can be made on a single sheet pan with minimal preparation. If you line your sheet pan with aluminum foil, you may even get away with not having to clean it!

30-Minute recipes: Dinner served in 30 minutes or less! Everything in these recipes, from the prep work to the cooking, takes no more than half an hour.

5-Ingredient recipes: These recipes use just 5 ingredients or fewer. (Oil, salt, and pepper are not counted toward the total.)

Many of these recipes fit into more than one of these categories, so you'll get quick, easy, healthy meals with minimal cleanup. If you set aside an hour or two at the beginning of the week to prep the ingredients for the week, you could have all the cooking done in even less time. When I said this cookbook was here to help, I meant it! Dreams do come true for us busy cooks.

WHAT NOT TO EAT (AND WHY)

It is extremely important to educate yourself about which foods contain gluten and be vigilant about what you put in your body. Accidentally making yourself sick is no fun. If you have celiac disease or another type of gluten intolerance, even very small amounts of gluten can cause symptoms like rashes, vomiting, diarrhea, joint and muscle pain, headaches, and more.

The main sources of gluten are wheat, barley, rye, and oats. (Oats are naturally gluten-free but are usually processed alongside wheat, barley, or rye, and get cross-contaminated in the process. Gluten-free-certified oats are safe to eat.) That means you'll find gluten in all the foods typically made with wheat: beer, bread, pasta, cereal, cookies, pastries, flour tortillas, bagels, and so on. Gluten is also used to process foods that wouldn't otherwise contain wheat, so you'll sometimes find it in sauces, salad dressings, condiments, ice cream, candy, chips, french fries, and even premade seasoning packets.

Always read the package labels before eating something, especially with those tricky foods that sometimes contain gluten. For example, salt-and-vinegar potato chips may seem safe because there's no gluten in potatoes, salt, or most types of vinegar, but they often use malt vinegar, which is made from barley and isn't distilled, and is thus not gluten-free. Even if you've been safely consuming a product for a while, keep checking the label periodically to make sure the company hasn't changed their production process or ingredients.

Another danger to watch out for is cross-contamination, which occurs when tiny particles of gluten find their way into a supposedly gluten-free food because it was prepared too close to food that does contain gluten. A single crumb can be enough to cause a reaction.

Cross-contamination is almost always a risk in restaurants. Don't expect servers or coworkers to know what you can and can't eat, even if you've already told them several times. The situation is getting better, but there are definitely still gaps in education. I was once served a salad that had a stray crouton in it. Even though I specifically told them about my allergy, they thought it would be fine to just pick off the croutons, not realizing that the whole salad had been contaminated. Gently educate people when possible, and hope that it'll help someone else in the future.

KITCHEN EQUIPMENT AND PANTRY ESSENTIALS

Even though I cook for a living, I believe in cooking with the bare minimum. Easy, natural recipes should be made with basic kitchen equipment. Here's the equipment I used while crafting the recipes in this book.

Must Have

- Large (6-quart) pot with lid
- Small and medium saucepans with lids
- Large nonstick pan
- Large baking sheet
- Muffin tin
- High-quality knife
- Cutting board
- Whisk
- Wooden spoon
- Spatulas
- Measuring cups, liquid and dry
- Measuring spoons

Nice to Have

- Stand or handheld mixer
- High-powered blender
- Immersion blender
- Aluminum foil
- Parchment paper
- Mason jars
- Slow cooker, Instant Pot, and/or pressure cooker

Similarly, a well-stocked pantry with the most basic ingredients can be transformed into some absolutely amazing dishes. You don't need extravagant ingredients to make delicious meals. Having these staples on hand at all times will make gluten-free eating so much easier, especially when you have to make dinner in a pinch! Here are some of my must-have pantry essentials.

Pantry Essentials

- Baking powder
- Baking soda
- Gluten-free all-purpose flour blend (Note: The nutritional information for the recipes in this cookbook was calculated using Bob's Red Mill Gluten-Free 1-to-1 Baking Flour; nutritional information may vary when using other brands.)
- Gluten-free certified rolled oats
- Chocolate chips
- Vanilla extract (see Two-Ingredient Vanilla Extract, page 133)
- Unsalted butter
- Olive oil
- Gluten-free pasta
- Gluten-free soy sauce
- Quinoa
- Rice
- Sea salt
- Black pepper
- Garlic powder
- Onion powder
- Chili powder

ABOUT THE RECIPES

As you read through this cookbook, you'll see labels indicating One-Pot or One-Pan, Sheet Pan, 30-Minute, 5-Ingredient recipes, or a combination of labels. Virtually all these recipes also include one or more helpful tips with additional advice. Want to know how best to make a recipe ahead of time or what ingredients to use to make a recipe dairy-free? These tips will provide that information.

Additionally, you'll see labels telling you if a recipe is in one of the following categories:

- **Vegetarian:** Contains no meat or seafood.
- **Vegan:** Contains no meat, seafood, dairy, eggs, or other animal products.
- **Nut-Free:** Contains no nuts.
- **Dairy-Free:** Contains no dairy.

The recipes in this cookbook are all about making our gluten-free lives easier. And all the recipes are meant for the entire family. They're delicious, simple to make, and enjoyable for everyone, gluten-free or not. They keep me happy and healthy, and I hope they do the same for you!

ALLERGY TRIGGERS and SUBSTITUTIONS

If you're prone to allergies, there are ingredients other than gluten out there that also can cause bad reactions. It's important to stay aware of what you're putting in your body. Here are the "big 8" allergens and some suggestions for substitutions.

GLUTEN: Use gluten-free flours made from grains like corn and rice instead of wheat, barley, and rye. My favorite is Bob's Red Mill Gluten-Free 1-to-1 Baking Flour; it's the best of everything I've tried.

DAIRY: The sugar lactose is what many react to in dairy. Replace dairy products with lactose-free alternatives; there are plenty of dairy-free milk, cheese, and yogurt products out there.

PEANUTS: If you're not allergic to tree nuts, go for nuts like cashews and almonds. If you're allergic to both, sunflower seed butter is a great alternative to peanut butter.

EGGS: You can often substitute flax "eggs," applesauce, or bananas in recipes that call for eggs—or use my personal favorite, Bob's Red Mill Egg Replacer.

SOY: You can make gluten-free, soy-free "soy" sauce at home using gluten-free broth, vinegar, and molasses. Or try coconut aminos, which imparts a similar flavor to most dishes.

FISH: To get the nutrients normally found in fish, try leafy green vegetables and flaxseed oil. There are also plenty of soy-based fishless products available if you're not allergic to soy.

SHELLFISH: As with fish, you can get your dose of healthy omega-3 fatty acids from other sources like leafy green vegetables and flaxseed oil.

TREE NUTS (CASHEWS, ALMONDS, WALNUTS, ETC.): If you're allergic to tree nuts *and* peanuts, opt for sunflower seeds and sunflower seed butter instead.

CHAPTER TWO

Smoothies and Breakfasts

BLUEBERRY BREAKFAST SMOOTHIES

I'm not a morning person, so this is my type of breakfast: quick, simple, and good for you, with almost zero thinking necessary. Just throw everything in the blender, and you get a smoothie that tastes like chocolate but is sweetened with antioxidant-rich blueberries and bananas instead of a bunch of refined sugar.

SERVES 2 / PREP TIME: 2 MINUTES

`5-INGREDIENTS` `30-MINUTES`

DAIRY-FREE

VEGAN

2 cups unsweetened almond milk

1 cup fresh spinach

1 banana

½ cup frozen blueberries

2 tablespoons unsweetened cocoa powder

1. In a blender, combine the milk, spinach, banana, blueberries, and cocoa powder.

2. Pulse for 30 to 45 seconds.

3. Serve immediately.

Per serving Calories 129; Fat 4g; Total Carbohydrates 24g; Fiber 6g; Sodium 194mg; Protein 3g

LEMON BAR OVERNIGHT OATMEAL

Obsessed with lemon bars? Me too. But they're too sugary to eat as often as I want to. Try this overnight oatmeal recipe and enjoy all the flavors of a lemon bar for breakfast, without the guilt.

SERVES 1 / PREP TIME: 5 MINUTES, PLUS 2 HOURS TO CHILL

NUT-FREE

VEGETARIAN

1 cup whole milk

½ cup gluten-free certified rolled oats

½ cup vanilla Greek yogurt

2 tablespoons freshly squeezed lemon juice

2 tablespoons honey

1 tablespoon grated lemon zest, plus more for topping if desired

1 tablespoon chia seeds

Optional toppings: Lemon curd, lemon zest, shredded coconut, coconut cream, and/or toasted almonds

1. In a mason jar, combine the milk, rolled oats, yogurt, lemon juice, honey, lemon zest, and chia seeds. Put the lid on the jar.

2. Chill in the refrigerator for at least 2 hours, or overnight.

3. Top with any of the optional toppings, or eat as is.

DAIRY-FREE TIP: Use nondairy milk and yogurt instead of the real thing.

Per serving Calories 503; Fat 16g; Total Carbohydrates 78g; Fiber 8g; Sodium 131mg; Protein 21g

CRANBERRY-ALMOND BREAKFAST COOKIES

If I had my way, I'd eat cookies for breakfast all the time. With this recipe, I can! These super simple cranberry-almond breakfast cookies are packed with protein, providing a healthy way to sneak cookies into your morning routine.

MAKES 12 COOKIES / PREP TIME: 10 MINUTES / COOK TIME: 10 MINUTES

SHEET PAN   30-MINUTES

DAIRY-FREE

VEGETARIAN

1 cup gluten-free certified rolled oats

½ cup unsweetened applesauce

½ cup peanut butter

3 tablespoons honey

½ teaspoon vanilla extract

¼ teaspoon sea salt

½ cup sliced almonds

½ cup dried cranberries

1. Preheat the oven to 350°F. Line a sheet pan with parchment.

2. In a medium mixing bowl, stir together the rolled oats and applesauce. Allow the mixture to sit for 2 to 3 minutes.

3. Stir in the peanut butter, honey, vanilla extract, and salt.

4. Fold in the sliced almonds and dried cranberries.

5. Spoon the dough onto the prepared sheet pan, about 1 tablespoon at a time, so that you get 12 cookies. Flatten the cookies with your fingers.

6. Bake for 10 minutes.

7. Allow the cookies to fully cool, then serve or store in an airtight container.

ALLERGEN TIP: If you're allergic to peanuts, use sunflower seed butter instead of peanut butter. You can also omit the almonds.

(1 Cookie) Calories 123; Fat 8g; Total Carbohydrates 11g; Fiber 2g; Sodium 89mg; Protein 4g

NO-BAKE CHOCOLATE CHIP BREAKFAST BALLS

I often need a quick breakfast, especially before a workout. With a little bit of sweetness and a nice hit of protein, these breakfast balls give me the energy I need to go for a run. They pair perfectly with a cup of tea. I also like to stick a few in a resealable bag and keep them on hand as a travel snack when I know I'm going to be on the go and might not have access to any gluten-free food.

MAKES 12 BALLS / PREP TIME: 5 MINUTES, PLUS 20 MINUTES TO CHILL

30-MINUTES

DAIRY-FREE

VEGETARIAN

1 cup gluten-free certified rolled oats

½ cup peanut butter

½ cup roasted salted peanuts

½ cup mini chocolate chips

¼ cup honey

½ teaspoon vanilla extract

Pinch salt

1. In a medium bowl, combine the oats, peanut butter, peanuts, chocolate chips, honey, vanilla extract, and salt and mix well.

2. Cover and refrigerate for 20 to 30 minutes.

3. Form the balls by scooping a tablespoon of the mixture and rolling it between your palms.

4. Store in an airtight container in the fridge for up to 5 days.

NUT-FREE TIP: Try sunflower seed butter and sunflower seeds instead of the peanut butter and peanuts.

(1 ball) Calories 179; Fat 11g; Total Carbohydrates 18g; Fiber 2g; Sodium 109mg; Protein 5g

PERFECTLY FLUFFY PANCAKES

Whipping up pancakes for your family is one of the best ways to spend a Saturday morning. These pancakes make the experience even better by keeping everything simple and, of course, gluten-free. Serve with your favorite gluten-free syrup or jam!

SERVES 4 / PREP TIME: 10 MINUTES / COOK TIME: 15 MINUTES

ONE-PAN   30-MINUTES

NUT-FREE

VEGETARIAN

1¾ cups all-purpose gluten-free flour blend

2 tablespoons sugar

1½ teaspoons baking powder

1 teaspoon baking soda

½ teaspoon salt

2 large eggs

1¼ cups whole milk

½ teaspoon vanilla extract

Vegetable oil, for greasing the pan

1. In a large bowl, whisk together the flour blend, sugar, baking powder, baking soda, and salt.

2. Make a well in the center and add the eggs, milk, and vanilla extract. Mix until smooth.

3. Heat a lightly oiled pan over medium-high heat.

4. Pour about ¼ cup of the batter into the pan for each pancake. Spread the batter with a spoon if you prefer thinner pancakes, but don't let them touch. You will need to work in several batches, depending on the size of your pan.

5. Cook until you see bubbles start to rise to the surface of the pancakes, about 2 minutes. Flip the pancakes and cook the other side for an additional 1 to 2 minutes. Transfer the pancakes to a plate and repeat with the remaining batter, adding more oil to the pan if necessary.

DAIRY-FREE TIP: Replace the whole milk with your nondairy milk of choice plus ½ teaspoon apple cider vinegar.

EGG-FREE TIP: Use an egg replacement instead of the real thing.

(3 pancakes if 12 pancakes made) Calories 234; Fat 12g; Total Carbohydrates 32g; Fiber 1g; Sodium 678mg; Protein 8g

ONE-BOWL BANANA BREAD

I grew up with a loaf of banana bread always on the kitchen counter. It was something my family often made to use up bananas before they went bad—and to keep a sweet but healthful treat on hand. I'm happy to say that hasn't changed. The only difference is that my version is gluten-free! The fact that you can prepare it in a single bowl seems to make it taste even better.

MAKES 1 LOAF / PREP TIME: 10 MINUTES / COOK TIME: 30 MINUTES

DAIRY-FREE

NUT-FREE

VEGETARIAN

Nonstick cooking spray

2 large bananas

1 large egg, lightly beaten

½ cup unsweetened applesauce

½ cup sugar

1 teaspoon sea salt

½ teaspoon vanilla extract

1 cup all-purpose gluten-free flour blend

1 teaspoon baking powder

1 teaspoon baking soda

1. Preheat the oven to 350°F. Lightly coat an 8½-by-4½-inch loaf pan with cooking spray.

2. In a medium mixing bowl, mash the bananas. Add the egg, applesauce, sugar, salt, and vanilla extract and mix well.

3. Sift the flour, baking powder, and baking soda into the bowl. Slowly whisk together.

4. Pour the batter into the prepared loaf pan. Bake for 30 to 32 minutes, or until an inserted toothpick comes out clean.

TIP: If you use an egg replacement instead of an egg, the dish will be both egg-free and vegan!

(1 slice, if there are 9 pieces in the loaf) Calories 130; Fat 1g; Total Carbohydrates 29g; Fiber 2g; Sodium 359mg; Protein 2g

BLUEBERRY MUFFINS

I grew up on blueberry muffins from a mix. It might very well be the first thing I actually learned to make growing up. Unfortunately, those muffin mixes are made with wheat flour, so I came up with this recipe as a way to get my nostalgia fix without eating any gluten. These muffins will take you right back to your childhood—minus any adverse gluten reactions.

MAKES 12 MUFFINS / PREP TIME: 10 MINUTES / COOK TIME: 20 MINUTES

ONE-PAN   30-MINUTES

NUT-FREE

VEGETARIAN

1½ cups all-purpose gluten-free flour blend

½ teaspoon baking soda

½ teaspoon salt

2 large eggs

¾ cup whole milk

½ cup sugar

3 tablespoons olive oil

1 tablespoon vanilla extract

1 cup fresh blueberries

1. Preheat the oven to 350°F. Line a muffin tin with paper liners.

2. In a medium bowl, whisk together the flour, baking soda, and salt.

3. Create a well in the center of the mixture and add the eggs, milk, sugar, olive oil, and vanilla extract. Stir until well combined.

4. Gently fold in the blueberries.

5. Pour the batter into the prepared muffin cups.

6. Bake for 18 to 22 minutes, or until an inserted toothpick comes out clean.

DAIRY-FREE TIP: Replace the milk with your nondairy milk of choice plus ½ teaspoon apple cider vinegar.

EGG-FREE TIP: Use an egg replacement in place of the eggs.

(1 muffin) Calories 285; Fat 6g; Total Carbohydrates 51g; Fiber 6g; Sodium 167mg; Protein 7g

TO-GO VEGETARIAN QUICHE BITES

These quiche bites were a regular in my household during the years when my husband had to get up at 4 a.m. for a very long commute to work. We began making a week's worth every Sunday so he could heat them up and get a good start to the day without expending too much mental energy. Because, really, who has time to think about eating when you're basically getting up in the middle of the night?

MAKES 12 BITES / PREP TIME: 10 MINUTES / COOK TIME: 30 MINUTES

ONE-PAN

DAIRY-FREE

NUT-FREE

VEGETARIAN

Nonstick cooking spray

8 large eggs

1 teaspoon garlic powder

¼ teaspoon salt

¼ teaspoon freshly ground black pepper

½ cup chopped fresh spinach

½ cup chopped cherry tomatoes

¼ cup chopped onion

1 small red potato, chopped

1. Preheat the oven to 350°F. Lightly coat a muffin tin with cooking spray.

2. In a medium bowl, whisk together the eggs, garlic powder, salt, and pepper.

3. Divide the spinach, tomatoes, onion, and potato evenly among the muffin cups.

4. Pour the egg mixture over the veggies.

5. Stir each quiche briefly with a toothpick.

6. Bake for 25 to 30 minutes, or until an inserted toothpick comes out clean.

TIP: Feel free to add mushrooms, bell peppers, or any other veggies your heart desires!

(3 quiche bites) Calories 183; Fat 10g; Total Carbohydrates 10g; Fiber 1g; Sodium 294mg; Protein 14g

HASH and SPINACH EGGS

Although I'm the one who cooks for a living, my husband is definitely the breakfast maker of our household. He's the one who can take credit for this healthy, easy, and filling breakfast, which he cooks almost every weekend. Simply add everything to a hot pan, and breakfast is served!

SERVES 4 / PREP TIME: 10 MINUTES / COOK TIME: 25 MINUTES

ONE-PAN   5-INGREDIENTS

DAIRY-FREE

NUT-FREE

VEGETARIAN

3 medium russet potatoes, well scrubbed

2 tablespoons olive oil

1 small onion, chopped

1 cup chopped fresh spinach

½ teaspoon garlic powder

4 large eggs

¼ teaspoon salt

¼ teaspoon freshly ground black pepper

1. Pierce each potato several times with a fork. Microwave them for about 8 minutes, or until tender.

2. Roughly chop the potatoes into ½-inch pieces.

3. Heat the olive oil in a large pan over medium-high heat. Add the potatoes, onion, spinach, and garlic powder. Cook, stirring frequently, for 5 to 6 minutes, or until the onion is tender.

4. Press the hash and spinach down evenly throughout the pan.

5. With a wooden spoon, make 4 shallow wells, and crack one egg into each.

6. Add the salt and pepper.

7. Cover the pan and cook for 10 minutes, or until the egg whites are set.

8. Serve immediately.

Per serving Calories 252; Fat 12g; Total Carbohydrates 27g; Fiber 4g; Sodium 234mg; Protein 9g

BREAKFAST TACOS

For a fun twist on the idea of a breakfast taco, this recipe uses pancakes instead of tortillas for the taco shells. You get the best of both breakfast worlds: the savory flavors of sausage and eggs, as well as the familiar buttery sweetness of pancakes. You can also freeze these, then quickly pop them in the microwave on those morning when you want a delicious, hearty break-fast but need to make it quick.

SERVES 4 / PREP TIME: 5 MINUTES

30-MINUTES

NUT-FREE

1 recipe Perfectly Fluffy Pancakes (page 16), using ½ cup batter for each pancake

6 cooked sausage links, roughly chopped

1 cup scrambled eggs

½ cup chopped tomatoes

¼ cup chopped scallions

¼ cup shredded Cheddar cheese

Fill each pancake "taco shell" with some of the cooked sausage, scrambled eggs, chopped tomatoes, scallions, and Cheddar cheese and serve.

DAIRY-FREE TIP: Instead of using whole milk for the pancakes, use your nondairy milk of choice plus ½ teaspoon apple cider vinegar, and use a nondairy cheese or omit the cheese from the tacos.

FREEZING TIP: If you plan to freeze these tacos, omit the tomatoes—they don't freeze well. Once you've filled the taco shells, fold them and pin each one in place with a toothpick. Wrap the tacos in paper towels, slip them into a resealable plastic bag, and freeze. When you're ready to eat them, wrap each taco in a wet paper towel and microwave for 1 minute, then flip the taco and microwave for another 30 seconds.

Per serving Calories 945; Fat 47g; Total Carbohydrates 93g; Fiber 10g; Sodium 1,683mg; Protein 38g

Strawberry-Cucumber Salad (page 28)

CHAPTER THREE

Soups and Salads

CREAM of CHICKEN SOUP

Many recipes for casseroles and pot pies call for cream of chicken soup, but canned varieties often contain gluten. You can make this easy gluten-free version at home to use in those recipes or just to enjoy on its own. The savory flavors make it a perfect family meal on a cold winter night.

SERVES 4 / PREP TIME: 5 MINUTES / COOK TIME: 15 MINUTES

ONE-POT   30-MINUTES

NUT-FREE

2 tablespoons unsalted butter

½ cup all-purpose gluten-free flour blend

2 ½ cups gluten-free chicken broth

1¼ cups whole milk

1 teaspoon salt

½ teaspoon freshly ground black pepper

½ teaspoon onion powder

½ teaspoon garlic powder

¼ teaspoon dried parsley

1. In a large saucepan, melt the butter over medium heat, then whisk in the flour blend.

2. Slowly whisk in the chicken broth, milk, salt, pepper, onion powder, garlic powder, and dried parsley. Whisking constantly, bring to a low boil.

3. Turn the heat down to low and stir constantly for 5 to 10 minutes, or until the mixture begins to thicken.

4. Remove from the heat. The soup will thicken more as it cools.

DAIRY-FREE TIP: Swap out the milk and butter for nondairy milk options. Coconut or cashew milk would work particularly well.

INGREDIENT TIP: Gluten is often present in store-bought broths and soups. Check the label to make sure your chicken broth is gluten-free.

Per serving Calories 233; Fat 14g; Total Carbohydrates 19g; Fiber 2g; Sodium 1,057mg; Protein 10g

CALDO DE POLLO

This dish is one I learned from my husband. When we first got together, he would compare every soup I made to caldo de pollo (Spanish for "chicken broth," though it's much more than mere broth). Finally I told him, "Let's stop comparing every soup to caldo and actually make it." And here it is! It's my husband's version of chicken noodle soup when he's sick.

SERVES 8 / PREP TIME: 10 MINUTES / COOK TIME: 2 HOURS

ONE-POT

DAIRY-FREE

NUT-FREE

10 cups water

3 cups gluten-free chicken broth

2 tablespoon minced garlic

2 large boneless, skinless chicken breasts

7 red potatoes, roughly chopped

1 medium onion, roughly chopped

2 cups baby carrots

10 cabbage leaves, roughly chopped

1 (28-ounce) can diced tomatoes

Pinch salt

Pinch freshly ground black pepper

1 lemon, cut into 8 wedges (optional)

1. In a large stockpot, combine the water, chicken broth, and garlic. Bring to a boil over medium-high heat.

2. Add the chicken breasts and reduce the heat to medium-low. Cook for 45 minutes.

3. Add the potatoes, onion, baby carrots, cabbage leaves, tomatoes with their juice, salt, and pepper.

4. Cover the pot and cook for another 45 minutes, or until the veggies are soft and the chicken is cooked through. The chicken will be starting to fall apart; you can shred it with a fork if you like.

5. If desired, squeeze fresh lemon juice into each bowl of soup just before serving.

INGREDIENT TIP: Gluten is present in many store-bought broths and soups. Check the label to make sure your chicken broth is gluten-free.

Per serving Calories 298; Fat 2g; Total Carbohydrates 40g; Fiber 6g; Sodium 197mg; Protein 32g

POTATO-BROCCOLI SOUP

My absolute favorite soup growing up was potato-broccoli. Quite often the store-bought versions contain gluten, but who cares when the homemade version tastes better and is such a breeze to make? With this recipe, you put in a few simple ingredients, and out comes this soup with a rich, creamy flavor.

SERVES 4 / PREP TIME: 15 MINUTES / COOK TIME: 30 MINUTES

ONE-POT

NUT-FREE

VEGETARIAN

2 tablespoons unsalted butter

1 small onion, finely chopped

6 cups chopped broccoli florets

2 large russet potatoes, peeled and diced

1 tablespoon minced garlic

2 cups gluten-free vegetable broth

2 cups whole milk

¼ teaspoon ground nutmeg (optional)

Pinch salt

Pinch freshly ground black pepper

1. In a large saucepan, melt the butter over medium heat. Add the onion and sauté for 2 to 3 minutes, or until soft.

2. Add the broccoli, potatoes, and garlic. Cover and cook for 5 minutes.

3. Add the vegetable broth and bring to a boil, then turn the heat back down to a simmer for 15 minutes, or until the vegetables are tender when pierced with a fork.

4. With an immersion blender, purée the vegetables until completely smooth or still a little chunky, depending on your preference.

5. Stir in the milk, nutmeg (if using), salt, and pepper.

6. Gently heat the soup over low heat for 5 to 8 minutes, or until heated through.

DAIRY-FREE TIP: Replace the butter and milk with nondairy substitutes. I recommend coconut butter and coconut milk for maximum creaminess.

INGREDIENT TIP: Gluten is often present in store-bought broths and soups. Check the label to make sure your vegetable broth is gluten-free.

Per serving Calories 314; Fat 10g; Total Carbohydrates 48g; Fiber 8g; Sodium 196mg; Protein 11g

CREAM of MUSHROOM SOUP

Cream of mushroom was never a favorite soup of mine growing up. What I didn't realize was that it always tasted awful because it always came from a can! I became a big fan of that creamy mushroom goodness once I realized that my homemade version was far superior (and, of course, entirely gluten-free). Now it's my staple when I'm not feeling well.

SERVES 4 / PREP TIME: 5 MINUTES / COOK TIME: 20 MINUTES

ONE-POT   30-MINUTES

NUT-FREE

4 tablespoons (½ stick) unsalted butter

12 ounces white mushrooms, finely chopped

¼ cup all-purpose gluten-free flour blend

2 cups gluten-free chicken broth

1⅓ cups whole milk

1 tablespoon freshly squeezed lemon juice

1 tablespoon dried parsley

Pinch salt

Pinch freshly ground black pepper

1. In a large saucepan, melt the butter over medium heat. Add the mushrooms and gently cook for 5 minutes.

2. Stir in the flour blend, then gradually add the broth.

3. Bring to a boil, then reduce the heat and simmer for 10 minutes.

4. Stir in the milk, lemon juice, parsley, salt, and pepper.

5. Gently heat the soup over low heat for 5 to 8 minutes, or until heated through. Serve immediately.

DAIRY-FREE TIP: Replace the butter and milk with nondairy substitutes. Coconut butter and coconut milk work best in a creamy soup like this one.

INGREDIENT TIP: Many store-bought broths and soups contain gluten. Check the label on your chicken broth to make sure it's gluten-free.

Per serving Calories 294; Fat 19g; Total Carbohydrates 20g; Fiber 2g; Sodium 281mg; Protein 13g

STRAWBERRY-CUCUMBER SALAD

This is one of my favorite go-to salads when company is over. It's simple and easy to make ahead of time, but the flavors are so complex: The sweet tartness of the strawberries, the acidity of the vinegar, and the creamy tang of the feta all complement each other perfectly, while the crunchy cucumber gives it a great mouthfeel.

SERVES 4 / PREP TIME: 10 MINUTES

30-MINUTES

NUT-FREE

VEGETARIAN

2 large cucumbers, sliced

2 cups sliced strawberries

½ medium onion, sliced

¼ cup balsamic vinegar

2 tablespoons
  mild olive oil

½ cup feta cheese

1. In a large bowl, toss together the cucumbers, strawberries, onion, balsamic vinegar, and olive oil.

2. Top with feta cheese before serving.

TIP: Omit the feta cheese for a dairy-free and vegan salad.

Per serving Calories 164; Fat 11g; Total Carbohydrates 13g; Fiber 3g; Sodium 214mg; Protein 4g

MASON JAR TACO SALAD

If there is one thing I will never tire of, it's taco salad. You get all the fantastic flavors of a taco, but without the carbs—or gluten—usually found in tortillas. This recipe lets you make multiple servings ahead of time and store them in mason jars, so you can get your taco salad fix on the go.

SERVES 5 / PREP TIME: 15 MINUTES / COOK TIME: 15 MINUTES

30-MINUTES

NUT-FREE

1 pound lean ground beef

¼ cup Homemade Taco Seasoning (page 126)

¼ cup water

1½ cups gluten-free salsa

5 tablespoons sour cream

1 quart cherry tomatoes, chopped

1 small onion, chopped

2 avocados, halved, pitted, peeled, and chopped

Juice of ½ lime

5 cups chopped romaine lettuce

1. In a medium pan, cook the ground beef over medium heat for 7 to 10 minutes, or until it's no longer pink. Drain off the grease.

2. Add the taco seasoning and water, and cook until most of the water evaporates. Allow the taco mixture to cool.

3. Divide the ingredients among 5 wide-mouth, 1-quart mason jars so that each contains the following layers in the following order: salsa, sour cream, tomatoes, onion, avocados, lime juice, taco mixture, lettuce.

4. Seal the jars and store in the refrigerator for up to 5 days.

5. When you're ready to eat, place the contents into a bowl—or just grab a fork and eat straight from the jar.

DAIRY-FREE TIP: Swap the sour cream for dairy-free plain yogurt.

INGREDIENT TIP: Some store-bought salsas contain gluten. Check the label on yours to make sure it's gluten-free.

Per serving Calories 512; Fat 26g; Total Carbohydrates 40g; Fiber 14g; Sodium 2,069mg; Protein 37g

LEMONY KALE SALAD with PARMESAN and GOLDEN RAISINS

My sister made this salad one day while I was visiting, and I was skeptical I'd like it. It seemed like one of those recipes that people insist tastes great but that really just tastes like kale. I'm so glad I was wrong. It ended up being the first time I ate raw kale and found myself enjoying it! Whether you love your leafy greens or you're a kale skeptic like me, you've got to try it.

SERVES 4 / PREP TIME: 5 MINUTES, PLUS 1 HOUR TO CHILL

5-INGREDIENTS

NUT-FREE

VEGETARIAN

6 cups chopped curly kale

¼ cup olive oil

Juice of 1 lemon

½ cup grated Parmesan cheese

½ cup golden raisins

1. In a large bowl, toss the kale with the olive oil and lemon juice.

2. Mix in the Parmesan cheese and golden raisins.

3. Refrigerate until chilled, about 1 hour.

TIP: Use a nondairy cheese or leave out the Parmesan cheese for a dairy-free and vegan salad.

Per serving Calories 257; Fat 16g; Total Carbohydrates 25g; Fiber 2g; Sodium 175mg; Protein 8g

EASY THREE-BEAN SALAD

Three kinds of beans is all you need! Throw them in a bowl, toss in some basic but delicious ingredients, and you have a fabulous dish to bring to a potluck or picnic. It's vegetarian (vegan if you leave out the honey), but absolutely packed with healthy protein.

SERVES 8 / PREP TIME: 15 MINUTES, PLUS 3 HOURS TO CHILL

DAIRY-FREE

NUT-FREE

VEGETARIAN

1 (15-ounce) can black beans, drained and rinsed

1 (15-ounce) can red kidney beans, drained and rinsed

1 (15-ounce) can chickpeas, drained and rinsed

½ medium red onion, finely chopped

½ cup apple cider vinegar

¼ cup honey

3 tablespoons olive oil

3 tablespoons dried parsley

1 teaspoon salt

½ teaspoon freshly ground black pepper

1. In a large bowl, toss together the black beans, kidney beans, chickpeas, and onion.

2. In a small bowl, whisk together the vinegar, honey, olive oil, parsley, salt, and pepper.

3. Pour the dressing over the beans and stir to coat. Cover and chill in the refrigerator for at least 3 hours or overnight.

TIP: If you're vegan (or watching your sugar intake), omit the honey.

Per serving Calories 266; Fat 6g; Total Carbohydrates 43g; Fiber 10g; Sodium 638mg; Protein 10g

MUSTARD POTATO SALAD

I absolutely love mustard, as will become very clear throughout this book. A good grainy mustard is such a simple way to add spicy, pungent flavor to a dish that needs a little oomph. It can also do wonders for a dish like this potato salad, where it balances beautifully with the olive oil and vinegar.

SERVES 4 / PREP TIME: 15 MINUTES, PLUS 4 HOURS TO CHILL / COOK TIME: 10 MINUTES

DAIRY-FREE

NUT-FREE

VEGAN

9 medium red potatoes, quartered

2½ cups chopped broccoli florets

1 small onion, chopped

½ cup gluten-free Dijon mustard

2 teaspoons olive oil

1 teaspoon gluten-free distilled white vinegar

Pinch salt

Pinch freshly ground black pepper

1. Fill a large pot with water and bring to a boil over high heat. Reduce the heat to low and add the potatoes and broccoli. Cook for 7 to 10 minutes, or until the potatoes are tender.

2. Drain the potatoes and broccoli in a colander and cool under cold running water.

3. In a large bowl, toss the cooled potatoes and broccoli with the onion.

4. In a small bowl, whisk together the mustard, olive oil, vinegar, salt, and pepper.

5. Pour the dressing over the potatoes and toss to coat.

6. Cover and chill in the refrigerator for at least 4 hours before serving.

INGREDIENT TIP: Most types of vinegar, including apple cider, red wine, and balsamic vinegar, are naturally gluten-free. Malt vinegar is not. Because it's distilled, white vinegar should be gluten-free, even if it's made from gluten-containing grains, but some people do report reacting to it, possibly because of cross-contamination at some point during production.

Per serving Calories 465; Fat 5g; Total Carbohydrates 95g; Fiber 16g; Sodium 502mg; Protein 17g

CLASSIC TUNA-MACARONI SALAD

This pasta salad never gets old. Really, it's one of those delicious dishes I'm always excited to make. It's not very often that I get to eat the ones people bring to potlucks and parties, so when I get to make and actually eat it, it's a real treat!

SERVES 6 / PREP TIME: 15 MINUTES, PLUS 1 HOUR TO CHILL / COOK TIME: 15 MINUTES

5-INGREDIENTS

DAIRY-FREE

NUT-FREE

2 cups gluten-free
  elbow macaroni

2 (4.5-ounce) cans
  albacore tuna, drained

1 (10-ounce) can
  peas, drained

1⅓ cups Homemade
  Mayonnaise (page 131)

3 tablespoons gluten-free
  sweet pickle relish

Pinch salt

Pinch freshly ground
  black pepper

1. Prepare the macaroni according to the package directions. Drain and rinse under cold running water.

2. Transfer the pasta to a medium bowl. Add the tuna, peas, mayonnaise, relish, salt, and pepper and mix well.

3. Cover and refrigerate until cold, about 1 hour.

HEALTH TIP: Replace the mayonnaise with Greek yogurt for a healthier option.

INGREDIENT TIP: Store-bought condiments can contain gluten. Check the label to make sure your relish and mayonnaise (if you use store-bought) are gluten-free.

Per serving Calories 497; Fat 35g; Total Carbohydrates 24g; Fiber 4g; Sodium 447mg; Protein 15g

Parmesan-Baked Asparagus (page 45)

CHAPTER FOUR

Simple Sides and Snacks

CRISPY SWEET POTATO FRIES with AIOLI DIP

Sweet potato fries are my husband's favorite. He orders them at restaurants whenever he can. With this recipe, he doesn't have to wait until we go out to eat—he can have them at home whenever a craving strikes. He prefers to eat them plain, but I like to dip them in a creamy, garlicky aioli sauce.

SERVES 4 / PREP TIME: 10 MINUTES / COOK TIME: 30 MINUTES, PLUS 25 MINUTES RESTING TIME

SHEET PAN

NUT-FREE

VEGETARIAN

FOR THE FRIES

3 sweet potatoes, well scrubbed and cut into 1-by-4-inch fries

2½ tablespoons gluten-free cornstarch

4 tablespoons (½ stick) unsalted butter, melted

½ teaspoon salt

½ teaspoon freshly ground black pepper

½ teaspoon garlic powder

FOR THE AIOLI

½ cup Homemade Mayonnaise (page 131)

1 tablespoon freshly squeezed lemon juice

½ teaspoon garlic powder

TO MAKE THE FRIES

1. Preheat the oven to 400°F. Line a rimmed sheet pan with aluminum foil.

2. In a large bowl, toss the sweet potatoes with the cornstarch.

3. Dump the sweet potatoes onto the prepared sheet pan, discarding any excess cornstarch.

4. Drizzle the butter over the fries, then sprinkle the salt, pepper, and garlic powder over them. Gently toss the fries and spread them out in a single layer.

5. Bake for 15 minutes.

6. Flip the fries over and bake for 12 more minutes.

7. Turn off the oven, but keep the sweet potatoes inside as the oven cools, about 25 minutes.

8. Serve with the aioli dipping sauce.

TO MAKE THE AIOLI

In a small bowl, whisk together the mayonnaise, lemon juice, and garlic powder.

DAIRY-FREE TIP: Replace the butter with a nondairy option.

INGREDIENT TIP: Store-bought condiments can contain gluten, and although cornstarch is naturally gluten-free, it's sometimes processed in plants where it can be cross-contaminated. Check the labels to make sure your cornstarch and mayonnaise (if you use store-bought) are gluten-free.

Per serving Calories 387; Fat 32g; Total Carbohydrates 25g; Fiber 3g; Sodium 607mg; Protein 2g

SMASHED GARLIC SWEET POTATOES

These smashed sweet potatoes drenched in garlic butter are a simple side dish. They taste almost decadent, but they're actually good for you, because sweet potatoes are packed with vitamins, fiber, and complex carbohydrates.

SERVES 4 / PREP TIME: 10 MINUTES / COOK TIME: 20 MINUTES

SHEET PAN   5-INGREDIENTS   30-MINUTES

DAIRY-FREE

NUT-FREE

VEGETARIAN

4 sweet potatoes, well scrubbed and cut crosswise into 2-inch-thick pieces

Nonstick cooking spray

4 tablespoons (½ stick) unsalted butter, melted

3 garlic cloves, minced

½ teaspoon salt

¼ cup chopped fresh chives, for garnish

1. Put the sweet potatoes in a large pot and cover with cool water. Bring the water to a boil over medium-high heat and cook the sweet potatoes for 10 to 12 minutes, or until they're tender when pierced with a fork. Drain.

2. Turn on the broiler. Lightly coat a rimmed sheet pan with cooking spray.

3. Transfer the sweet potatoes to the sheet pan and gently smash them so that they flatten a bit but still stay together.

4. In a small bowl, whisk together the butter and garlic.

5. Brush the butter mixture onto each smashed sweet potato. Sprinkle with the salt.

6. Broil for 5 to 8 minutes, or until the sweet potatoes are slightly charred.

7. Garnish with the fresh chives and serve immediately.

DAIRY-FREE TIP: Instead of butter, use a dairy-free option like coconut butter.

Per serving Calories 218; Fat 12g; Total Carbohydrates 27g; Fiber 4g; Sodium 444mg; Protein 2g

CREAMY MASHED POTATOES

If I could survive on nothing but mashed potatoes, I would. Seriously. It runs in the family. We all love our potatoes, and we'll pair these Creamy Mashed Potatoes with any fabulous, comforting meal.

SERVES 6 / PREP TIME: 10 MINUTES / COOK TIME: 25 MINUTES

ONE-POT   5-INGREDIENTS

NUT-FREE

VEGETARIAN

12 russet potatoes, peeled and chopped

4 tablespoons (½ stick) unsalted butter

¼ cup whole milk

2 teaspoons onion powder

1. Put the potatoes in a large pot and cover with cool water. Bring the water to a boil over medium-high heat and cook the potatoes for 20 to 25 minutes, or until they're tender when pierced with a fork.

2. Reserving ¼ cup of the cooking water, drain the potatoes, then immediately return them to the pot, along with the reserved cooking water. (You can also just drain most of the water but not all of it, reserving about ¼ cup.)

3. Add the butter, milk, and onion powder.

4. Manually mash the potatoes, or use an immersion blender to blend until smooth.

5. Serve immediately.

DAIRY-FREE TIP: Replace the butter and milk with nondairy alternatives like coconut butter and coconut milk.

Per serving Calories 371, Fat 9g, Total Carbohydrates 68g; Fiber 10g; Sodium 85mg; Protein 8g

PARMESAN-ROASTED POTATO WEDGES

Roasted Potatoes and Parmesan go together like PB&J. If you love potatoes and Parmesan these Parmesan-Roasted Potato Wedges are for you!

ERVES 4 / PREP TIME: 5 MINUTES / COOK TIME: 35 MINUTES

SHEET PAN   **5-INGREDIENTS**

NUT-FREE

VEGETARIAN

4 large red potatoes,
  cut into wedges

2 tablespoons olive oil

1 tablespoon salt

¼ cup freshly grated
  Parmesan cheese

1. Preheat the oven to 450°F. Line a rimmed sheet pan with aluminum foil.

2. Toss the potato wedges with the olive oil and salt on the sheet pan. Spread out the wedges in a single layer.

3. Bake for 30 minutes.

4. Sprinkle the Parmesan cheese over the wedges and bake for 5 more minutes.

5. Serve immediately.

DAIRY-FREE TIP: Replace the Parmesan cheese with a nondairy substitute.

Per serving Calories 341; Fat 9g; Total Carbohydrates 59g; Fiber 6g; Sodium 1,832mg; Protein 9g

LOADED POTATO SKINS

Making these potato skins is a breeze, and people love them every time. They're a great nosh for when you're having company over. Or forget about company—this is an entirely acceptable snack to keep all for yourself.

SERVES 5 / PREP TIME: 15 MINUTES / COOK TIME: 25 MINUTES

SHEET PAN

NUT-FREE

5 medium russet potatoes, well scrubbed

¼ cup olive oil

½ teaspoon salt

¼ teaspoon freshly ground black pepper

¾ cup shredded Cheddar cheese

¼ cup chopped cooked bacon

¼ cup sour cream

¼ cup chopped scallion

1. Preheat the oven to 400°F.

2. Pierce each potato with a fork several times, and microwave on high for 10 to 12 minutes.

3. Let the potatoes cool for 10 minutes, then cut them in half lengthwise and scoop out the insides with a spoon (reserve the potato flesh for another use).

4. Brush the potatoes inside and out with the olive oil. Sprinkle with the salt and pepper.

5. Place the potatoes, skin-side up, on a rimmed sheet pan and bake for 8 minutes.

6. Flip the potatoes over and fill them with the Cheddar cheese and bacon. Bake for another 5 minutes.

7. Garnish each potato skin with a dollop of sour cream and some scallions before serving.

TIP: Use nondairy plain Greek yogurt instead of sour cream and nondairy cheese instead of Cheddar. Leave out the bacon for a hearty vegan snack.

Per serving Calories 363; Fat 25g; Total Carbohydrates 25g; Fiber 2g; Sodium 696mg; Protein 12g

SLOW COOKER BAKED BEANS

I know I'm not the only one who loves baked beans, especially paired with coleslaw at a summer barbecue. This recipe is especially easy: You just throw all the ingredients into the slow cooker, then sit back and wait while your kitchen fills with heavenly aromas.

SERVES 12 / PREP TIME: 10 MINUTES / COOK TIME: 1½ TO 3 HOURS

ONE-POT

DAIRY-FREE

NUT-FREE

4 (15-ounce) cans small red beans, drained and rinsed

6 slices bacon, cooked and crumbled

1 cup finely chopped onion

½ cup finely chopped green bell pepper

1 cup gluten-free ketchup

½ cup (packed) brown sugar

2 tablespoons gluten-free maple syrup

2 teaspoons gluten-free mustard

1½ teaspoons garlic powder

1 teaspoon apple cider vinegar

½ teaspoon salt

½ teaspoon freshly ground black pepper

1. Combine the beans, bacon, onion, bell pepper, ketchup, brown sugar, maple syrup, mustard, garlic powder, vinegar, salt, and pepper in a slow cooker and mix well.

2. Cover and cook on low for 3 hours or on high for 1½ hours.

VEGAN TIP: For a vegan version of this dish, just leave out the bacon.

INGREDIENT TIP: Many store-bought condiments contain gluten. Check the labels on your ketchup, mustard, and syrup to make sure they're gluten-free.

Per serving Calories 256; Fat 5g; Total Carbohydrates 42g; Fiber 10g; Sodium 992mg; Protein 13g

SWEET BUTTER-ROASTED CARROTS

A couple years back, my husband finally broke down and realized he needed to eat more vegetables. I knew he'd need to take baby steps into the wonderful world of vegetables, and these carrots were just the thing. With just a little bit of butter and honey, this recipe can make a vegetable lover out of even the most stubborn carnivore.

SERVES 4 / PREP TIME: 5 MINUTES / COOK TIME: 20 MINUTES

SHEET PAN   5-INGREDIENTS   30-MINUTES

NUT-FREE

VEGETARIAN

1 pound carrots, peeled and cut into 3-inch pieces (about 4 cups)

2 tablespoons unsalted butter, melted

2 tablespoons honey

½ teaspoon salt

¼ teaspoon freshly ground black pepper

1. Preheat the oven to 425°F. Line a rimmed sheet pan with aluminum foil.

2. Toss together the carrots, butter, honey, salt, and pepper on the sheet pan. Spread out the carrots in a single layer.

3. Bake for 18 to 20 minutes, or until the carrots are fork-tender.

4. Serve immediately.

DAIRY-FREE TIP: Instead of butter, try nondairy options like coconut butter.

Per serving Calories 130; Fat 6g; Total Carbohydrates 20g; Fiber 3g; Sodium 410mg; Protein 1g

SIMPLE ROASTED BROCCOLI

I fell in love with roasted broccoli years back, and it's been a long-term love relationship ever since. This recipe is so easy to quickly throw into the oven whenever you need a healthy and delicious side to pair with any meal.

SERVES 4 / PREP TIME: 5 MINUTES / COOK TIME: 25 MINUTES

SHEET PAN	5-INGREDIENTS	30-MINUTES

NUT-FREE

VEGETARIAN

1 pound broccoli florets, cut into bite-size pieces

2 tablespoons olive oil

1 teaspoon salt

1 teaspoon freshly ground black pepper

¼ cup freshly grated Parmesan cheese

1. Preheat the oven to 350°F.

2. Spread out the broccoli florets in a single layer on a rimmed sheet pan. Drizzle with the olive oil and sprinkle with the salt and pepper.

3. Bake for 25 to 30 minutes, or until the broccoli is tender.

4. Sprinkle the Parmesan cheese on top and serve immediately.

DAIRY-FREE TIP: Instead of Parmesan cheese, try nutritional yeast.

Per serving Calories 123; Fat 9g; Total Carbohydrates 8g; Fiber 3g; Sodium 685mg; Protein 6g

PARMESAN-BAKED ASPARAGUS

I'm all about roasted vegetables, if you haven't noticed by now. It has always been my favorite way to eat my veggies, and this recipe is a great example. Even people who don't think they like asparagus will love it.

SERVES 4 / PREP TIME: 10 MINUTES / COOK TIME: 10 MINUTES

SHEET PAN   5-INGREDIENTS   30-MINUTES

NUT-FREE

VEGETARIAN

1 pound asparagus, trimmed

2 tablespoons olive oil

½ cup grated Parmesan cheese

½ teaspoon garlic powder

¼ teaspoon salt

¼ teaspoon freshly ground black pepper

1 lemon, quartered, for garnish

1. Preheat the oven to 400°F.

2. Toss together the asparagus, olive oil, Parmesan cheese, garlic powder, salt, and pepper on a rimmed sheet pan. Spread out the asparagus in an even layer.

3. Bake for 10 to 12 minutes, or until the asparagus is tender.

4. Garnish each serving with a lemon wedge and additional Parmesan cheese, if you wish.

DAIRY-FREE TIP: Replace the Parmesan cheese with a nondairy alternative.

Per serving Calories 130; Fat 10g; Total Carbohydrates 5g; Fiber 2g; Sodium 281mg; Protein 7g

QUICK DROP BISCUITS

I was practically raised on drop biscuits. After I had to go gluten-free, it was years before I realized how much I missed them—such a homey, satisfying food for so little effort. Once I perfected this recipe, though, there was a drop biscuit marathon. I paired a biscuit with every meal, even breakfast. Here's hoping you'll enjoy a biscuit boom of your own.

SERVES 6 / PREP TIME: 10 MINUTES / COOK TIME: 15 MINUTES

SHEET PAN   30-MINUTES

NUT-FREE

VEGETARIAN

2 cups all-purpose gluten-free flour blend

2 tablespoons sugar

2 teaspoons baking powder

1 teaspoon salt

½ teaspoon baking soda

8 tablespoons (1 stick) unsalted butter, chilled and cubed

2 large eggs

½ cup whole milk

1. Preheat the oven to 425°F. Lightly grease a rimmed sheet pan.

2. In a large bowl, whisk together the flour blend, sugar, baking powder, salt, and baking soda.

3. Cut in the cold butter with your fingers or a pastry blender, blending until the mixture resembles coarse crumbs.

4. Add the eggs and milk and mix just until combined; do not overmix.

5. Drop the batter by the spoonful onto the prepared sheet pan.

6. Bake for 13 to 15 minutes, or until the tops are golden brown. Serve immediately.

DAIRY-FREE TIP: Swap out the butter and milk in favor of nondairy substitutes.

Per serving Calories 328; Fat 18g; Total Carbohydrates 35g; Fiber 4g; Sodium 634mg; Protein 7g

CHEESY JALAPEÑO CORNBREAD MUFFINS

I'm seriously obsessed with cornbread—which is very convenient, because corn is gluten-free! Add cheese and jalapeño peppers to the mix, and spicy, cheesy, heavenly cornbread muffins are born.

MAKES 12 MUFFINS / PREP TIME: 10 MINUTES / COOK TIME: 25 MINUTES

ONE-PAN

NUT-FREE

VEGETARIAN

3 tablespoons unsalted butter, melted

2 large eggs

1 cup whole milk

¼ cup honey

1 teaspoon gluten-free cornstarch

½ teaspoon salt

½ teaspoon baking soda

1 cup gluten-free cornmeal

½ cup all-purpose gluten-free flour blend

⅓ cup shredded Cheddar cheese

1 jalapeño pepper, seeded and diced

1. Preheat the oven to 350°F. Line a muffin tin with paper liners.

2. In a large mixing bowl, whisk together the melted butter, eggs, milk, and honey.

3. Whisk in the cornstarch, salt, and baking soda.

4. Whisk in the cornmeal and flour blend.

5. Stir in the Cheddar cheese.

6. Pour the mixture evenly into the prepared muffin cups.

7. Top each muffin with a piece of jalapeño pepper.

8. Bake for 20 to 25 minutes, or until an inserted toothpick comes out clean.

DAIRY-FREE TIP: Feel free to swap out the butter, milk, and cheese in favor of nondairy substitutes.

INGREDIENT TIP: Corn is naturally gluten-free, but cornmeal and cornstarch are often processed in plants that also process wheat and other sources of gluten, which presents a contamination risk. Check the label to make sure your cornstarch is gluten-free.

(1 muffin) Calories 112; Fat 6g; Total Carbohydrates 13g; Fiber 1g; Sodium 210mg; Protein 3g

JALAPEÑO POPPERS

Even as someone whose ability to handle spicy food is kind of pathetic, I absolutely love jalapeño poppers! The key is to use cream cheese to tamp down the heat. If your spice tolerance is low like mine, you might also want to prepare yourself with a glass of milk—but you'll still be totally addicted! My family goes gaga over these every time.

MAKES 12 POPPERS / PREP TIME: 10 MINUTES / COOK TIME: 30 MINUTES

ONE-PAN   5-INGREDIENTS

NUT-FREE

VEGETARIAN

12 jalapeño peppers

8 ounces cream cheese, at room temperature

2 teaspoons garlic powder

1 teaspoon paprika

1. Preheat the oven to 400°F.

2. Slit the jalapeños lengthwise down one side. Scrape out the seeds with a small spoon.

3. In a small bowl, mix the cream cheese, garlic powder, and paprika.

4. Spoon 1 tablespoon of the cream cheese mixture into each jalapeño.

5. Place the jalapeños side by side in a 9-by-13-inch baking dish and bake for 30 minutes. Serve immediately.

DAIRY-FREE TIP: Swap out the cream cheese for a nondairy cream cheese substitute.

(2 poppers) Calories 148; Fat 14g; Total Carbohydrates 4g; Fiber 1g; Sodium 847mg; Protein 4g

HAM, CREAM CHEESE, and DILL PICKLE ROLL-UPS

These delightful roll-ups are a food from my childhood, but my mother hardly ever made them. The only time we got our hands on them was during big family get-togethers, so I've always thought of them as a rare treat for special occasions. But now I can make them anytime I want! I love them for quick lunches, and they're still a hit when I take them to a party.

SERVES 4 / PREP TIME: 15 MINUTES

5-INGREDIENTS   30-MINUTES

NUT-FREE

4 ounces cream cheese

6 ounces sliced ham

½ cup dill pickle spears

3 scallions, cut into
  3-inch pieces

1. Spread 1 tablespoon of cream cheese on each slice of ham.

2. Place a pickle and scallion at one end of each ham slice and roll it up into a tube shape.

3. Cut each roll-up into 4 pieces. Secure with toothpicks, if desired.

DAIRY FREE TIP: Just use nondairy cream cheese.

Per serving Calories 174; Fat 14g; Total Carbohydrates 4g; Fiber 1g; Sodium 874mg; Protein 10g

BACON-WRAPPED DATES

I don't know why, but every time I make these as an appetizer or snack, people are skeptical about them. Of course, as soon as they pop one in their mouth, they're raving about the taste and asking me for the recipe. What I love most about them is that they look so fancy, even though they're ridiculously easy to make. It's an entertainer's dream.

SERVES 4 / PREP TIME: 15 MINUTES / COOK TIME: 20 MINUTES

SHEET PAN   **5-INGREDIENTS**

NUT-FREE

18 pitted dates

5 ounces goat cheese

9 slices bacon, cut
in half crosswise

1. Preheat the oven to 350°F. Line a rimmed baking sheet with parchment paper.

2. Make a slit halfway into each date to create an opening. Spoon a small amount of goat cheese into each date and press it closed.

3. Wrap each date in a half-slice of bacon, and secure with a toothpick.

4. Place the dates in a single layer on the prepared sheet pan and bake for 10 to 15 minutes; then flip the dates over and bake for another 5 to 10 minutes, or until the bacon is crisped to your liking.

Per serving Calories 431; Fat 26g; Total Carbohydrates 29g; Fiber 3g; Sodium 1,118mg; Protein 23g

THREE-INGREDIENT PEANUT BUTTER FRUIT DIP

Dunk some fresh fruit in this dip for a naturally sweet, protein-packed snack, at home or at a party. It's so good that sometimes I just eat it with a spoon. Use whatever vessel you need to get it in your tummy!

SERVES 4 / PREP TIME: 5 MINUTES

5-INGREDIENTS   30-MINUTES

VEGETARIAN

½ cup vanilla Greek yogurt

½ cup peanut butter

¼ cup honey

1. In a small bowl, whisk together the Greek yogurt, peanut butter, and honey.

2. Store in an airtight container in the fridge.

DAIRY-FREE TIP: Simply swap in nondairy yogurt.

Per serving Calories 290; Fat 18g; Total Carbohydrates 28g; Fiber 2g; Sodium 166mg; Protein 9g

Sweet Potato Mexican Lasagna (page 62)

CHAPTER FIVE

Vegan and Vegetarian Main Dishes

GARLIC BUTTER NOODLES

This is one of those meals I began making when I was in college and wanted flavorful food that wouldn't cost too much money. I might not be a poor college student anymore, but to be honest, it's still one of my favorite dishes to make. It features all my favorite simple but delicious flavors, tossed with some noodles. If you do eat dairy, I highly recommend using the Parmesan cheese, as it takes this dish to a whole new level.

SERVES 4 / PREP TIME: 5 MINUTES / COOK TIME: 5 MINUTES

ONE-PAN   5-INGREDIENTS   30-MINUTES

NUT-FREE

VEGETARIAN

1 tablespoon olive oil

¼ cup minced garlic

8 tablespoons (1 stick) unsalted butter

½ teaspoon salt

½ teaspoon freshly ground black pepper

4 cups cooked gluten-free pasta of your choice

1 cup grated Parmesan cheese (optional)

1. In a medium pan, heat the olive oil over medium heat. Add the garlic and cook for 2 minutes.

2. Add the butter and let it melt. Add the salt and pepper.

3. Fold in the pasta, stirring until it's covered in sauce.

4. Sprinkle with the Parmesan cheese and serve immediately.

DAIRY-FREE TIP: Omit the cheese or use a nondairy cheese, and replace the butter with a nondairy equivalent.

Per serving Calories 718; Fat 34g; Total Carbohydrates 94g; Fiber 1g; Sodium 719mg; Protein 16g

SPICY BLACK BEAN BURGERS

I came up with this recipe many years back, and my husband has been requesting it regularly ever since. Many store-bought veggie burgers contain gluten (and lots of the other questionable ingredients), so being able to make these at home is a win!

MAKES 4 PATTIES / PREP TIME: 20 MINUTES, PLUS 1 HOUR TO CHILL / COOK TIME: 10 MINUTES

DAIRY-FREE

NUT-FREE

VEGETARIAN

2 tablespoons olive oil, divided

⅓ cup quinoa

⅔ cup water

1 (15-ounce) can black beans, drained and rinsed

2 large eggs

½ cup gluten-free bread crumbs

¼ cup minced fresh parsley

4 garlic cloves, roughly chopped

3 tablespoons onion powder

1½ teaspoons ground cumin

¼ teaspoon salt

¼ teaspoon freshly ground black pepper

1. In a small saucepan, heat 1 tablespoon of olive oil over medium heat. Add the quinoa and cook, stirring often, for 3 to 4 minutes.

2. Add the water and bring to a boil, then reduce the heat to low, cover, and cook for 15 to 20 minutes, or until the quinoa is fully cooked and fluffy.

3. Transfer the quinoa to a food processor. Add the black beans, eggs, bread crumbs, parsley, garlic, onion powder, cumin, salt, and pepper. Pulse 4 or 5 times, or until the mixture is fully combined but is not puréed.

4. Cover and refrigerate for at least 1 hour.

5. Form the mixture into 4 patties.

6. In a large pan, heat the remaining 1 tablespoon of oil over medium-high heat. Cook the patties for 3 to 5 minutes on each side, or until seared on the outside and heated through.

SERVING TIP: Serve on gluten-free hamburger buns with gluten-free condiments and your favorite burger toppings.

(1 patty) Calories 250; Fat 11g; Total Carbohydrates 28g; Fiber 6g; Sodium 286mg; Protein 11g

SIMPLE VEGAN BOLOGNESE SAUCE

This recipe provides all the goodness of a hearty, chunky Bolognese sauce without any meat (or the gluten you might find in store-bought varieties). As a bonus, it's perfect for leftovers—as delicious as it is the day you make it, let it sit overnight, and the flavors evolve into something even more rich and wonderful!

SERVES 6 / PREP TIME: 15 MINUTES / COOK TIME: 15 MINUTES

ONE-POT   30-MINUTES

DAIRY-FREE

NUT-FREE

VEGAN

2 tablespoons olive oil

1 onion, chopped

½ cup chopped peeled carrot

1 cup chopped mushrooms

2 tablespoons minced garlic

1 (28-ounce) can crushed tomatoes

1 (6-ounce) can gluten-free tomato paste

3 tablespoons dry red wine (optional)

1 tablespoon dried basil

1 tablespoon dried oregano

1 tablespoon dried thyme

1 tablespoon dried parsley

1 teaspoon red pepper flakes

¼ teaspoon salt

¼ teaspoon freshly ground black pepper

6 cups cooked gluten-free pasta of your choice

1. In a large saucepan, heat the olive oil over medium heat. Add the onion, carrot, mushrooms, and garlic and sauté for 5 minutes, or until the vegetables begin to soften.

2. Add the crushed tomatoes, tomato paste, red wine (if using), basil, oregano, thyme, parsley, red pepper flakes, salt, and pepper. Bring the mixture to a simmer and cook for 10 minutes.

3. Serve over your favorite gluten-free pasta.

INGREDIENT TIP: Store-bought tomato paste is usually, but not always, gluten-free. Check the label to be sure.

Per serving Calories 549; Fat 6g; Total Carbohydrates 116g; Fiber 9g; Sodium 391mg; Protein 12g

SWEET POTATO-SPINACH LASAGNA

Lasagna may seem like a heavy dish, but it can be good for you if you pack it with healthy ingredients! I love hiding vegetables in comfort foods. This lasagna is a perfect example of that.

SERVES 8 / PREP TIME: 15 MINUTES / COOK TIME: 30 MINUTES

NUT-FREE

VEGETARIAN

Nonstick cooking spray

2 sweet potatoes, peeled and chopped

3 cups fresh baby spinach

3 cups ricotta cheese

1 tablespoon dried oregano

2 teaspoons garlic powder

½ teaspoon salt

½ teaspoon freshly ground black pepper

12 gluten-free lasagna noodles (uncooked)

1 (24-ounce) jar gluten-free marinara sauce

½ cup shredded mozzarella cheese

1. Preheat the oven to 375°F. Lightly coat a 9-by-13-inch baking dish with cooking spray.

2. In a food processor, pulse together the sweet potatoes and baby spinach until well chopped and combined but not puréed. Stir in the ricotta cheese, oregano, garlic powder, salt, and pepper.

3. Start with a layer of lasagna noodles in the bottom of the prepared baking dish, followed by a layer of the ricotta mixture, and finally a layer of sauce. Continue making layers until all the ingredients are gone, ending with noodles on top.

4. Cover with aluminum foil. Bake for 25 to 30 minutes, or until bubbly.

5. Scatter the mozzarella cheese over the top. Bake, uncovered, for another 5 minutes, or until the cheese is melted.

DAIRY-FREE TIP: Replace the ricotta and mozzarella with nondairy substitutes.

INGREDIENT TIP: Store-bought sauces can contain gluten. Check the label to make sure your marinara sauce is gluten-free.

Per serving Calories 311; Fat 11g; Total Carbohydrates 37g; Fiber 4g; Sodium 673mg; Protein 17g

ROASTED ROOT VEGETABLES with MAPLE and APPLE CIDER VINAIGRETTE

This recipe has it all: hearty root vegetables, tangy apple cider vinegar, and sweet maple syrup. Put it all together, and this side dish might even steal center stage from the main course.

SERVES 4 / PREP TIME: 10 MINUTES / COOK TIME: 20 MINUTES

SHEET PAN   30-MINUTES

DAIRY-FREE

NUT-FREE

VEGAN

Nonstick cooking spray

¼ cup olive oil

3 tablespoons apple cider vinegar

1 tablespoon gluten-free maple syrup

1 tablespoon gluten-free Dijon mustard

½ teaspoon sea salt

½ teaspoon freshly ground black pepper

6 carrots, peeled and halved lengthwise

8 garlic cloves, lightly smashed

2 medium onions, cut into ¼-inch-thick slices

4 red potatoes, quartered

1. Preheat the oven to 375°F. Line a rimmed sheet pan with aluminum foil and coat the foil with cooking spray.

2. In a small bowl, whisk together the olive oil, vinegar, maple syrup, Dijon mustard, salt, and pepper.

3. Combine the carrots, garlic cloves, onions, and potatoes on the prepared sheet pan. Drizzle the vinaigrette over the vegetables and gently toss to coat. Spread out the vegetables in a single layer.

4. Bake for 20 minutes, or until the potatoes are tender when pierced with a fork.

INGREDIENT TIP: Store-bought condiments can contain gluten. Check the labels on your syrup and mustard to be sure they're gluten-free.

Per serving Calories 344; Fat 13g; Total Carbohydrates 54g; Fiber 7g; Sodium 359mg; Protein 6g

QUINOA and BLACK BEAN TACOS with LIME

These tacos are quick, easy, healthy, and packed with flavor. Even my meat-eating husband loves this vegan recipe! I think it's because of the magic flavor you get when you mix the lime and slight spice from the red pepper flakes. You and your family will enjoy that magic, too!

SERVES 4 / PREP TIME: 10 MINUTES / COOK TIME: 20 MINUTES

ONE-POT   30-MINUTES

DAIRY-FREE

NUT-FREE

VEGAN

1 tablespoon olive oil

1 small red onion, chopped

2 tablespoons minced garlic

1 cup water

½ cup quinoa

1 teaspoon ground cumin

½ teaspoon red pepper flakes

1 (15-ounce) can black beans, drained and rinsed

¼ cup freshly squeezed lime juice

½ teaspoon salt

¼ teaspoon freshly ground black pepper

6 to 8 small corn tortillas, warmed

1 small avocado, halved, pitted, peeled, and sliced

1. In a medium pot, heat the olive oil over medium heat. Add the onion and garlic and sauté for about 4 minutes, or until the onions turn translucent.

2. Add the water, quinoa, cumin, and red pepper flakes.

3. Bring the water to a boil, then reduce the heat, cover, and simmer for 12 to 15 minutes, or until the quinoa is fully cooked and fluffy.

4. Stir in the black beans, lime juice, salt, and pepper.

5. Spoon the quinoa mixture into the warm corn tortillas, top with the avocado slices, and serve.

INGREDIENT TIP: If you're not vegan or dairy free, try sprinkling some Monterey Jack cheese on top of your tacos.

Per serving Calories 363; Fat 16g; Total Carbohydrates 48g; Fiber 12g; Sodium 394mg; Protein 11g

QUINOA-SPINACH-STUFFED TOMATOES with MARINARA SAUCE

These tomatoes are vegetarian (vegan if you leave out the cheese), but they're stuffed with quinoa and spinach for plenty of healthy protein and iron. They're versatile enough to serve as a side or as a main course.

SERVES 4 / PREP TIME: 15 MINUTES / COOK TIME: 40 MINUTES

ONE-POT

NUT-FREE

VEGETARIAN

Nonstick cooking spray

8 medium tomatoes

2 cups water

1 cup quinoa

1 tablespoon olive oil

5 cups fresh baby spinach

3 tablespoons minced garlic

1 teaspoon dried parsley

½ teaspoon salt

½ teaspoon freshly ground black pepper

1 cup gluten-free marinara sauce

½ cup shredded mozzarella cheese

¼ cup grated Parmesan cheese

1. Preheat the oven to 375°F. Lightly coat a 9-by-13-inch baking dish with cooking spray.

2. Cut a thin slice off the stem end of each tomato and scoop out the insides. If necessary, cut a thin slice off the bottom of each tomato to allow them to sit upright.

3. Place the tomatoes in the prepared baking dish.

4. In a small saucepan, bring the water to a boil. Stir in the quinoa and olive oil. Lower the heat, cover, and simmer for 12 to 15 minutes, or until the quinoa is fully cooked and fluffy.

5. Stir in the spinach, garlic, parsley, salt, and pepper.

6. Fill the hollowed-out tomatoes with the quinoa mixture.

7. Spoon 2 tablespoons of marinara sauce over each tomato.

8. Cover the baking dish with aluminum foil and bake for 18 to 20 minutes, or until the tomatoes are tender.

9. Remove the foil, scatter the mozzarella and Parmesan over the tomatoes, and bake for 5 more minutes.

DAIRY-FREE TIP: Replace the cheese with nondairy substitutes, or leave it out entirely—the quinoa provides plenty of protein.

INGREDIENT TIP: Store-bought sauces can contain gluten. Check the label to make sure your marinara sauce is gluten-free.

Per serving Calories 337; Fat 11g; Total Carbohydrates 50g; Fiber 9g; Sodium 679mg; Protein 14g

SWEET POTATO MEXICAN LASAGNA

This lasagna variant is where comfort food meets health food. It's filled with sweet potatoes, black beans, and corn tossed in a spicy-sweet taco sauce, and uses naturally gluten-free corn tortillas instead of lasagna noodles. It's a perfect weeknight dinner (with leftovers for lunch).

SERVES 8 / PREP TIME: 20 MINUTES / COOK TIME: 1 HOUR

NUT-FREE

VEGETARIAN

Nonstick cooking spray

2 large sweet potatoes, peeled and chopped

1 medium white onion, chopped

1 green bell pepper, seeded and chopped

2 tablespoons olive oil

3 tablespoons Homemade Taco Seasoning (page 126)

1 (15-ounce) can corn, drained

1 (15-ounce) can black beans, drained and rinsed

1 cup Best Taco Sauce Ever (page 127), divided

9 to 11 small corn tortillas

1 (15-ounce) can vegetarian refried beans

2 cups gluten-free enchilada sauce

½ cup shredded Cheddar cheese

1. Preheat the oven to 350°F. Lightly coat a rimmed sheet pan with cooking spray.

2. Combine the sweet potato, onion, and bell pepper on the prepared sheet pan. Toss with the olive oil and taco seasoning to coat. Spread the vegetables out in a single layer. Bake for 20 minutes.

3. Transfer the cooked vegetables to a large bowl. Add the corn, black beans, and ½ cup of taco sauce and mix well.

4. Pour the remaining ½ cup of taco sauce into the bottom of a 9-by-13-inch baking dish.

5. Start with a layer of corn tortillas on top of the taco sauce, followed by a layer of the vegetable mixture, then the refried beans, and finally the enchilada sauce. Continue making layers until all the ingredients are gone, ending with corn tortillas on top.

6. Cover with aluminum foil. Bake for 25 to 30 minutes, or until bubbly and the cheese is melted.

7. Remove the foil and scatter the cheese over the top. Bake for an additional 5 minutes, or until the cheese is melted.

DAIRY-FREE TIP: Replace the cheese with nondairy substitutes, or omit it entirely.

INGREDIENT TIP: Store-bought sauces can contain gluten. Check the label on your enchilada sauce (and your taco sauce if you use store-bought) to make sure it's gluten-free.

Per serving Calories 598; Fat 16g; Total Carbohydrates 96g; Fiber 19g; Sodium 1,645mg; Protein 22g

VEGAN SHEPHERD'S PIE

Shepherd's pie is a classic comfort food creation, with a naturally gluten-free crust of potatoes instead of pastry. It's designed to give you everything you need in a single filling dish: meat, potatoes, and vegetables. This vegan twist gets rid of the meat and replaces dairy with coconut products, but it's still comfort food at its finest!

SERVES 8 / PREP TIME: 15 MINUTES / COOK TIME: 1 HOUR

DAIRY-FREE

NUT-FREE

VEGAN

6 large russet potatoes, peeled and quartered

2 tablespoons coconut oil

¼ cup coconut milk

1 teaspoon salt, divided

1 teaspoon freshly ground black pepper, divided

1 tablespoon olive oil

1 pound white mushrooms

1 small onion, chopped

2 cups chopped peeled carrots

2 cups frozen peas

1 cup canned petite diced tomatoes

2 teaspoons garlic powder

1 teaspoon dried basil

1 teaspoon gluten-free Italian seasoning

¼ cup gluten-free vegetable broth

2 tablespoons gluten-free cornstarch

1. Put the potatoes in a large pot and cover with cool water. Bring the water to a boil over medium-high heat and cook the potatoes for 20 to 25 minutes, or until they're tender when pierced with a fork. Drain and return the potatoes to the pot.

2. Using an immersion blender, purée the potatoes, then mix in the coconut oil, coconut milk, ½ teaspoon of salt, and ½ teaspoon of pepper.

3. Preheat the oven to 350°F.

4. Heat the olive oil in a 4-quart Dutch oven over medium heat. Sauté the mushrooms, onion, and carrots for 3 to 5 minutes, or until they're tender.

5. Stir in the peas, tomatoes, garlic powder, basil, Italian seasoning, and the remaining ½ teaspoon of salt and ½ teaspoon of pepper.

6. In a small bowl, whisk together the vegetable broth and cornstarch.

7. Pour the cornstarch mixture into the vegetable mixture.

8. Spoon the mashed potatoes over the pie filling. Place the lid on the Dutch oven and bake for 35 minutes.

Per serving Calories 328; Fat 8g; Total Carbohydrates 58g; Fiber 11g; Sodium 385mg; Protein 10g

ENCHILADA STUFFED PORTOBELLOS

A plant-based recipe you can make in under 30 minutes, with Mexican flavors and minimal cleanup? This is my kind of dinner! These stuffed mushrooms make for a healthy but perfectly fulfilling dinner.

SERVES 3 / PREP TIME: 10 MINUTES / COOK TIME: 10 MINUTES

SHEET PAN   5-INGREDIENTS   30-MINUTES

NUT-FREE

VEGETARIAN

Nonstick cooking spray

2 tablespoons olive oil

6 portobello mushrooms, stems removed

1 cup canned or frozen (thawed) corn

1 cup canned black beans

½ teaspoon salt

1½ cups gluten-free enchilada sauce

½ cup shredded mozzarella cheese

1. Preheat the oven to 400°F. Lightly coat a rimmed sheet pan with cooking spray.

2. Brush the olive oil over the mushrooms and place them, stemmed side up, on the prepared sheet pan.

3. Divide the corn and black beans evenly among the mushroom caps.

4. Season with the salt and drizzle the enchilada sauce evenly over the mushrooms.

5. Top with the shredded cheese.

6. Bake for 8 to 12 minutes, or until the stuffing is hot and the portobellos are tender.

DAIRY-FREE TIP: Replace the cheese with a nondairy alternative, or omit it entirely—there's still plenty of flavor without it!

INGREDIENT TIP: Store-bought sauces can contain gluten. Check the label to make sure your enchilada sauce is gluten-free.

Per serving Calories 226; Fat 11g; Total Carbohydrates 25g; Fiber 5g; Sodium 645mg; Protein 12g

BEST-EVER VEGETABLE FRIED RICE

Oh my word, I absolutely love vegetable fried rice, especially how quick and easy it is to throw together. I keep a batch of cooked rice in my fridge at all times so I can make this dish whenever I want. I've experimented with other versions containing slightly harder-to-find ingredients, but the recipe I'm sharing with you is the classic, made with ingredients you probably already have on hand.

SERVES 8 / PREP TIME: 10 MINUTES / COOK TIME: 10 MINUTES

30-MINUTES

NUT-FREE

VEGETARIAN

1 teaspoon olive oil

1 small onion, chopped

2 cups chopped carrots

2 cups frozen peas

1 teaspoon garlic powder

½ teaspoon ground ginger

½ teaspoon salt

3 large eggs

2 cups hot cooked brown rice

¼ cup gluten-free soy sauce

2 tablespoons unsalted butter

1. In a large pan, heat the olive oil over medium heat. Add the onion and carrots and sauté until the onion is translucent, about 4 minutes.

2. Add the peas, garlic powder, ginger, and salt. Push the vegetables to one side of the pan.

3. In a small bowl, whisk together the eggs, then pour them into the open side of the pan.

4. Scramble the eggs and cook for 3 to 4 minutes. Stir the scrambled eggs into the veggies.

5. Add the rice, soy sauce, and butter.

6. Stir-fry for 1 minute to allow the butter to melt. Remove from the heat and serve.

DAIRY-FREE TIP: Use a nondairy alternative to butter.

INGREDIENT TIP: Store-bought soy sauce usually contains gluten. Make sure you get gluten-free soy sauce.

Per serving Calories 190; Fat 6g; Total Carbohydrates 27g; Fiber 4g; Sodium 684mg; Protein 7g

SPICY BLACK BEAN NACHOS

The black bean dip in this recipe is super healthy for you and even works great as a dip for veggies. But it's really at its best when you pile it onto corn tortilla chips with some cheese. Then you've got a quick comfort food win that's great to serve to a crowd or on date night.

SERVES 8 / PREP TIME: 15 MINUTES / COOK TIME: 15 MINUTES

30-MINUTES

NUT-FREE

VEGETARIAN

FOR THE BLACK BEAN DIP

2 teaspoons olive oil

½ white onion, chopped

3 garlic cloves, minced

1 (15-ounce) can black beans, drained and rinsed

½ cup water

¼ cup gluten-free salsa

½ teaspoon ground cumin

½ teaspoon salt

½ teaspoon freshly ground black pepper

FOR THE NACHOS

Nonstick cooking spray

5 cups corn tortilla chips

½ cup gluten-free salsa

1 cup shredded Monterey Jack cheese

¼ cup sliced jalapeño peppers

¼ cup sliced black olives

TO MAKE THE BLACK BEAN DIP

1. In a small saucepan, heat the olive oil over medium-high heat. Sauté the onion and garlic for 5 to 6 minutes, or until the onion is tender.

2. Transfer the sautéed onion and garlic to a food processor. Add the black beans, water, salsa, ground cumin, salt, and pepper. Pulse multiple times until the black bean dip is smooth.

TO MAKE THE NACHOS

1. Preheat the oven to 400°F. Lightly coat a 9-by-13-inch baking dish with cooking spray.

2. Spread out the tortilla chips in the bottom of the prepared baking dish. Spoon the black bean dip onto the chips, then spoon on the salsa. Scatter the cheese over the top, and finish with the jalapeño slices and black olives.

3. Bake for 5 to 7 minutes, or until the cheese is melted. Serve hot.

DAIRY-FREE TIP: You can't have nachos without cheese, but nondairy cheese works just fine!

INGREDIENT TIP: Some store-bought salsas contain gluten. Check the label on yours to make sure it's gluten-free.

Per serving Calories 188; Fat 10g; Total Carbohydrates 19g; Fiber 5g; Sodium 543mg; Protein 7g

TURMERIC-ROASTED VEGETABLES

Turmeric is known for its anti-inflammatory properties, and as many people with celiac disease know, any help with inflammation is welcome. Combine that with some delicious and healthy sweet potatoes, green beans, and chickpeas, and you've got a one-pan dinner win.

SERVES 4 / PREP TIME: 10 MINUTES / COOK TIME: 45 MINUTES

SHEET PAN   5-INGREDIENTS

DAIRY-FREE

NUT-FREE

VEGAN

3 sweet potatoes, peeled
   and chopped

4 tablespoons olive
   oil, divided

2 ½ teaspoons ground
   turmeric, divided

½ teaspoon salt, divided

½ teaspoon freshly ground
   black pepper, divided

3 cups green beans

1 (15-ounce) can chickpeas,
   drained and rinsed

1. Preheat the oven to 375°F. Line a rimmed sheet pan with aluminum foil.

2. Spread out the sweet potatoes on the prepared sheet pan. Drizzle with 2 tablespoons of olive oil, 1 teaspoon of turmeric, ¼ teaspoon of salt, and ¼ teaspoon of pepper. Toss to coat, and spread out the sweet potatoes in a single layer.

3. Cover the sheet pan with aluminum foil and bake for 20 to 25 minutes, or until the sweet potatoes are tender when pierced with a fork.

4. Add the green beans and chickpeas to the same sheet pan. Drizzle with the remaining 2 tablespoons of olive oil, 1½ teaspoons of turmeric, ¼ teaspoon of salt, and ¼ teaspoon of pepper. Toss everything to coat and spread the veggies out in a single layer.

5. Bake, uncovered, for another 20 to 22 minutes, or until the vegetables are fork-tender.

Per serving Calories 311; Fat 15g; Total Carbohydrates 40g; Fiber 7g; Sodium 462mg; Protein 7g

KALE and MUSHROOM QUINOA

This recipe can be eaten on its own or paired with the Turmeric-Roasted Vegetables (page 68); like those roasted vegetables, this quinoa dish is full of delicious and anti-inflammatory turmeric. It's perfect for lunch.

SERVES 4 / PREP TIME: 10 MINUTES / COOK TIME: 30 MINUTES

ONE-POT   5-INGREDIENTS

DAIRY-FREE

NUT-FREE

VEGAN

3 tablespoons olive oil, divided

10 ounces button mushrooms, chopped

3 cups finely chopped stemmed kale

2 tablespoons minced garlic

1 cup quinoa

2 cups water

1 tablespoon ground turmeric

½ teaspoon salt

½ teaspoon freshly ground black pepper

1. In a medium saucepan, heat 1 tablespoon of olive oil over medium heat. Add the mushrooms, kale, and garlic and sauté for 5 minutes.

2. Transfer the cooked vegetables to a bowl.

3. In the same saucepan, heat the remaining 2 tablespoons of olive oil over medium heat. Add the quinoa and cook the quinoa for 5 minutes.

4. Add the water and bring to a boil, then reduce the heat, cover, and simmer for 12 to 15 minutes, or until the water is absorbed and the quinoa is completely cooked.

5. Stir in the cooked vegetables, turmeric, salt, and pepper. Heat over low heat for 3 to 4 minutes to reheat the vegetables.

Per serving Calories 299; Fat 14g; Total Carbohydrates 38g; Fiber 5g; Sodium 320mg; Protein 10g

VEGAN SLOPPY JOES

This one-pot wonder is a plant-based take on an American classic. For this vegan variant, you'll pack your sloppy Joes with even more veggies (I'm always hiding as many vegetables as possible in my dishes), along with a sweet and tangy sloppy Joe sauce.

SERVES 4 / PREP TIME: 10 MINUTES / COOK TIME: 30 MINUTES

ONE-POT

DAIRY-FREE

NUT-FREE

VEGAN

1 tablespoon olive oil

1 large yellow onion, finely chopped

1 green bell pepper, seeded and finely chopped

2 tablespoons minced garlic

1 (6-ounce) can gluten-free tomato paste

1 (8-ounce) can gluten-free tomato sauce

2 cups cooked lentils

1 tablespoon gluten-free yellow mustard

2 teaspoons apple cider vinegar

2 teaspoons brown sugar

1½ teaspoons chili powder

½ teaspoon salt

½ teaspoon freshly ground black pepper

¼ teaspoon cayenne pepper

1 bay leaf

4 gluten-free hamburger buns, for serving

1. In a large saucepan, heat the olive oil over medium heat. Add the onion, bell pepper, and garlic and cook for 5 minutes.

2. Add the tomato paste, tomato sauce, lentils, mustard, vinegar, sugar, chili powder, salt, black pepper, cayenne, and bay leaf. Stir to combine.

3. Bring the mixture to a boil, then reduce the heat, cover, and simmer for 25 minutes.

4. Remove the bay leaf and serve on your favorite gluten-free buns.

INGREDIENT TIP: Store-bought sauces and condiments can contain gluten. Check the labels to make sure your tomato sauce, tomato paste, and mustard are gluten-free.

Per serving Calories 490; Fat 10g; Total Carbohydrates 85g; Fiber 24g; Sodium 1,027mg; Protein 22g

VEGETARIAN MEATLOAF

Before I learned about gluten, I spent several years as a vegetarian in an effort to cure my symptoms. During that time, there was one dish I really missed: meatloaf. I've never been a huge meat eater, so you'd think something like meatloaf would be the thing I missed least. But I love everything about this comfort food, especially topped with gluten-free ketchup and a big side of Creamy Mashed Potatoes (page 39). You can still get that comfort, even if you're a vegetarian, with this plant-based "meatloaf."

SERVES 6 / PREP TIME: 15 MINUTES / COOK TIME: 1 HOUR

DAIRY-FREE

NUT-FREE

VEGETARIAN

Nonstick cooking spray

1 teaspoon olive oil

½ cup finely chopped red onion

2 tablespoons minced garlic

1 cup grated carrot

½ cup grated red bell pepper

½ cup grated green bell pepper

1 (15-ounce) can black beans, drained and rinsed

1 cup cooked quinoa

½ cup gluten-free cornmeal

2 large eggs, lightly beaten

¼ cup gluten-free ketchup, plus 2 tablespoons, divided

1 teaspoon salt

1 teaspoon freshly ground black pepper

1. Preheat the oven to 400°F. Lightly coat an 8½-by-4½-inch loaf pan with cooking spray.

2. In a pan, heat the olive oil over medium heat. Add the onion, garlic, carrot, and bell peppers, and cook for 8 to 10 minutes, or until the veggies are soft.

3. In a large bowl, mash the black beans. Mix in the cooked veggies, quinoa, cornmeal, eggs, ¼ cup of ketchup, salt, and pepper.

4. Transfer the mixture to the prepared loaf pan. Spread the remaining 2 tablespoons of ketchup on top of the loaf.

5. Bake for 45 to 55 minutes, or until an inserted toothpick comes out clean.

INGREDIENT TIP: Store-bought condiments can contain gluten, and although cornmeal is naturally gluten-free, it's sometimes processed in plants where it can be contaminated. Check the labels to make sure your ketchup and cornmeal are gluten-free.

Per serving Calories 398; Fat 5g; Total Carbohydrates 70g; Fiber 14g; Sodium 600mg; Protein 21g

Fish Tacos with Pineapple-Mango Salsa (page 77)

CHAPTER SIX

Fish and Poultry Main Dishes

TUNA-STUFFED AVOCADO MELTS

This dish is packed with protein and healthy fats. If you make the tuna salad ahead of time on a Sunday devoted to meal prep, you can pop it into an avocado half (or between two slices of your favorite gluten-free bread) at a moment's notice. The cheesy melt really sends it over the top of deliciousness, but you can pack a cold version in your lunchbox, too—the creamy avocado and satisfying tuna salad are really all you need.

SERVES 2 / PREP TIME: 15 MINUTES / COOK TIME: 5 MINUTES

SHEET PAN   30-MINUTES

NUT-FREE

1 (4.5-ounce) can albacore tuna, drained

½ cup plain Greek yogurt

¼ cup minced celery

2 tablespoons gluten-free yellow mustard

2 tablespoons freshly squeezed lemon juice

½ teaspoon onion powder

¼ teaspoon freshly ground black pepper

2 avocados, halved, pitted, and peeled

½ cup shredded Cheddar cheese

1. Turn on the broiler.

2. In a small bowl, mix the tuna, Greek yogurt, celery, mustard, lemon juice, onion powder, and pepper until well combined.

3. Spoon the tuna salad into the centers of the avocado halves. Sprinkle the cheese on top.

4. Place the stuffed avocados on a small rimmed sheet pan.

5. Broil on high for 3 to 5 minutes, or until the cheese has melted. Serve immediately.

DAIRY-FREE TIP: Replace the cheese and yogurt with nondairy substitutes, or omit them entirely—the avocado is plenty creamy on its own.

Per serving Calories 698; Fat 54g; Total Carbohydrates 27g; Fiber 15g; Sodium 294mg; Protein 34g

LEMON-OLIVE OIL PASTA with TUNA

With its fresh ingredients and citrus kick, this dish just screams summer to me. I like to cook up some pasta on a Sunday so I can pull this meal together at the last minute later in the week. Enjoy it on the patio or at a picnic!

SERVES 4 / PREP TIME: 10 MINUTES / COOK TIME: 10 MINUTES

ONE-POT   **30-MINUTES**

DAIRY-FREE

NUT-FREE

1 teaspoon extra-virgin
   olive oil, plus ¼ cup,
   divided

3 tablespoons
   minced garlic

1 (4.5-ounce) can albacore
   tuna, drained

¼ teaspoon salt

¼ teaspoon freshly ground
   black pepper

4 cups cooked gluten-free
   spaghetti

Juice of 1 lemon

1 bunch parsley, stems
   removed and leaves
   roughly chopped

1. In a large saucepan, heat 1 teaspoon of olive oil over medium heat. Add the garlic and cook for 1 to 2 minutes, or until fragrant.

2. Add the tuna, salt, and pepper. Cook until heated through, 5 to 7 minutes.

3. Add the cooked pasta, lemon juice, parsley, and remaining ¼ cup of olive oil. Stir well. Serve immediately.

COOKING TIP: Once you've cooked your spaghetti, run it under cold water for 1 to 2 minutes. This not only stops it from cooking further but also removes the excess starch that generally accumulates with gluten-free pasta, so it won't stick together in a mushy clump when it cools.

Per serving Calories 368; Fat 15g; Total Carbohydrates 45g; Fiber 6g; Sodium 187mg; Protein 14g

KALE-SALMON CAESAR SALAD

Salads sometimes get a bad rap, but I love them because of recipes like this one. It's quick to pull together, filling, and a delicious way to use canned protein like salmon.

SERVES 2 / PREP TIME: 5 MINUTES

5-INGREDIENTS   30-MINUTES

NUT-FREE

5 cups chopped stemmed kale

1 (6-ounce) can salmon, drained

⅔ cup gluten-free Caesar salad dressing

½ cup shredded Parmesan cheese

¼ teaspoon salt

¼ teaspoon freshly ground black pepper

In a large bowl, gently toss together the kale, salmon, Caesar dressing, Parmesan cheese, salt, and pepper. Serve immediately.

TIP: Store-bought salad dressings can contain gluten. Check the label to make sure your Caesar dressing is gluten-free.

Per serving Calories 428; Fat 26g; Total Carbohydrates 20g; Fiber 3g; Sodium 876mg; Protein 32g

FISH TACOS with PINEAPPLE-MANGO SALSA

I'll admit it took me some time to jump on the fish taco bandwagon. Something about putting seafood in tacos always seemed, well, fishy to me (pun intended). But it's good to try new things, because once I did, oh my word, that flaky fish with pineapple-mango salsa captured my heart! It's definitely something you've got to try!

SERVES 4 / PREP TIME: 5 MINUTES, PLUS 30 MINUTES TO MARINATE / COOK TIME: 5 MINUTES

DAIRY-FREE

NUT-FREE

FOR THE SALSA

1 cup chopped mango

1 cup chopped pineapple

½ cup finely chopped red onion

1 jalapeño pepper, seeded and minced

¼ cup chopped fresh cilantro

Juice of 1 lime

Pinch salt

FOR THE TACOS

¼ cup olive oil

¼ cup chopped fresh cilantro

Juice of 1 lime

1 jalapeño pepper, seeded and minced

1 pound mahi-mahi fillets

8 corn tortillas

TO MAKE THE SALSA

In a small bowl, stir together the mango, pineapple, onion, jalapeño pepper, cilantro, lime juice, and salt. Cover and refrigerate until serving time.

TO MAKE THE TACOS

1. In a small bowl, whisk together the olive oil, cilantro, lime juice, and jalapeño.

2. Put the fish in a medium bowl. Pour the olive oil mixture over it and let it marinate for about 30 minutes.

3. Heat a pan over medium-high heat. Remove the fish from the marinade and cook on one side for 4 to 5 minutes, then flip and cook for an additional 1 minute.

4. Transfer the fish to a plate and flake with a fork.

5. Fill the corn tortillas with the flaked fish and top with the fresh salsa.

Per serving Calories 391; Fat 15g; Total Carbohydrates 41g; Fiber 5g; Sodium 163mg; Protein 25g

CHICKEN SALAD-STUFFED AVOCADOS

Chicken salad is another childhood favorite, so I had to find a way to eat it after going gluten-free. This recipe works great for chicken salad sandwiches made with gluten-free bread, but I like to put it in an avocado instead. I also use Greek yogurt instead of the traditional mayonnaise, for a slightly healthier version of comfort food. You'll be surprised—you really can't taste the difference.

SERVES 2 / PREP TIME: 10 MINUTES

30-MINUTES

NUT-FREE

2 cups chopped
  cooked chicken

½ cup plain Greek yogurt

¼ cup minced celery

2 tablespoons yellow
  mustard

1 teaspoon onion powder

¼ teaspoon freshly ground
  black pepper

2 avocados, halved, pitted,
  and peeled

1. In a small bowl, mix the chicken, Greek yogurt, celery, mustard, onion powder, and black pepper.

2. Spoon the chicken salad into the centers of the avocado halves.

DAIRY-FREE TIP: Use a nondairy alternative to Greek yogurt.

Per serving Calories 687; Fat 47g; Total Carbohydrates 23g; Fiber 14g; Sodium 307mg; Protein 48g

SHEET-PAN PARMESAN CHICKEN *with* GREEN BEANS

Parmesan chicken used to be my go-to order when eating out. These days, cross-contamination makes it too risky to order at a restaurant, but it's so easy to make at home—only one pan to clean!—that I don't mind.

SERVES 4 / PREP TIME: 10 MINUTES / COOK TIME: 30 MINUTES

`SHEET PAN`

NUT-FREE

Nonstick cooking spray

1 cup gluten-free cornmeal

¼ cup gluten-free Italian seasoning

¼ cup shredded Parmesan cheese

¼ teaspoon salt

4 boneless, skinless chicken breasts

4 cups cut green beans

2 teaspoons olive oil

1 cup gluten-free marinara sauce

½ cup shredded mozzarella cheese

1. Preheat the oven to 400°F. Line a rimmed sheet pan with aluminum foil and lightly coat the foil with cooking spray.

2. In a small bowl, whisk together the cornmeal, Italian seasoning, Parmesan cheese, and salt.

3. Coat the chicken breasts with the cornmeal mixture.

4. Place the chicken breasts on one half of the prepared sheet pan and the green beans on the other.

5. Drizzle the olive oil on the green beans, along with any leftover cornmeal mixture. Toss gently to coat.

6. Bake for 20 minutes.

7. Reduce the oven temperature to 350°F.

8. Spoon the marinara sauce over the chicken and sprinkle with the mozzarella. Bake for another 10 to 15 minutes, or until the chicken is cooked through and no longer pink.

9. Serve immediately.

INGREDIENT TIP: Store-bought sauces and seasoning packets are usually, but not always, gluten-free. Check the labels on your cornmeal, marinara sauce, and Italian seasoning to make sure they're gluten-free.

Per serving Calories 402; Fat 9g; Total Carbohydrates 48g; Fiber 9g; Sodium 1,527mg; Protein 35g

SHEET-PAN HONEY-GARLIC CHICKEN and VEGETABLES

Anytime you see "honey" *and* "garlic" in the title of a recipe, you know it's gotta be good. This recipe definitely is, with its mixture of sweet and savory flavors. Another weeknight wonder dinner here—just throw it on the sheet pan and let the magic happen.

SERVES 4 / PREP TIME: 10 MINUTES / COOK TIME: 35 MINUTES

SHEET PAN

DAIRY-FREE

NUT-FREE

Nonstick cooking spray

4 boneless, skinless
   chicken breasts

2 teaspoons garlic powder

½ teaspoon salt, divided

½ teaspoon freshly ground
   black pepper, divided

½ cup honey

¼ cup minced garlic

¼ cup gluten-free
   chicken broth

3 cups broccoli florets

4 red potatoes,
   cut in quarters

2 teaspoons olive oil

1. Preheat the oven to 400°F. Line a rimmed sheet pan with aluminum foil and lightly coat the foil with cooking spray.

2. On the sheet pan, season the chicken with the garlic powder, ¼ teaspoon of salt, and ¼ teaspoon of pepper.

3. In a small bowl, whisk together the honey, minced garlic, chicken broth, remaining ¼ teaspoon of salt, and remaining ¼ teaspoon of pepper.

4. Scatter the broccoli and potatoes around the chicken breasts on the sheet pan. Pour the honey-garlic mixture over the chicken and vegetables.

5. Drizzle the olive oil over the veggies.

6. Cover the sheet pan with aluminum foil and bake for 30 to 35 minutes, or until the chicken is completely cooked through and no longer pink.

7. Serve immediately.

INGREDIENT TIP: Store-bought broths and soups can contain gluten. Check the label to make sure your chicken broth is gluten-free.

Per serving Calories 452; Fat 5g; Total Carbohydrates 77g; Fiber 6g; Sodium 577mg; Protein 32g

SHEET-PAN BALSAMIC CHICKEN and ROASTED BROCCOLI

My fellow balsamic vinegar lovers out there will adore this easy and fulfilling recipe. Bonus: Balsamic vinegar is naturally gluten-free. And baking everything on a single sheet pan means you get a full meal of vegetables and protein, but with super easy cleanup!

SERVES 4 / PREP TIME: 5 MINUTES, PLUS 30 MINUTES TO MARINATE / COOK TIME: 35 MINUTES

SHEET PAN   5-INGREDIENTS

DAIRY-FREE

NUT-FREE

¼ cup olive oil

¼ cup balsamic vinegar

¼ cup minced garlic

½ teaspoon salt

½ teaspoon freshly ground black pepper

4 boneless, skinless chicken breasts

Nonstick cooking spray

4 cups broccoli florets

1. In a medium bowl, whisk together the olive oil, balsamic vinegar, garlic, salt, and pepper. Add the chicken and marinate in the refrigerator for about 30 minutes.

2. Preheat the oven to 400°F. Line a rimmed sheet pan with aluminum foil and lightly coat it with cooking spray.

3. Transfer the chicken to one half of the prepared sheet pan and put the broccoli on the other half. Pour the marinade over both the chicken and the broccoli.

4. Cover the sheet pan with aluminum foil and bake for 30 to 35 minutes, or until the chicken is completely cooked through and no longer pink.

5. Serve immediately.

COOKING TIP: The chicken is really best when marinated for 30 minutes, but if you're pressed for time, you can skip this step.

Per serving Calories 265; Fat 15g; Total Carbohydrates 9g; Fiber 3g; Sodium 532mg; Protein 28g

CRISPY BAKED CHICKEN FINGERS

Avoid that unhealthy frying oil and take these crispy gluten-free chicken fingers to a whole new level by baking them in the oven. It's not just better for you, it's also so much easier than frying. (If you haven't figured it out yet, I am a huge advocate of meals that require less work but still end up healthy and tasty.)

SERVES 4 / PREP TIME: 10 MINUTES / COOK TIME: 15 MINUTES

30-MINUTES

NUT-FREE

1 cup gluten-free
  fine cornmeal

½ teaspoon paprika

½ teaspoon salt

2 large eggs

¼ cup whole milk

1 pound thin chicken strips

¼ cup gluten-free
  cornstarch

1. Preheat the oven to 375°F. Line a rimmed sheet pan with parchment paper.

2. In a small bowl, mix the cornmeal and paprika.

3. In a separate bowl, whisk together the eggs and milk.

4. Put the chicken strips and cornstarch in a resealable plastic bag. Seal the bag and shake until the chicken strips are dusted with the starch.

5. Dip the dusted chicken strips in the egg mixture, then dredge them through the cornmeal mixture.

6. Place the strips in a single layer on the prepared sheet pan.

7. Bake for 6 minutes, then flip the strips over and bake for another 6 to 9 minutes, or until the chicken is cooked through and crispy.

COOKING TIP: For an even crispier coating, place the breaded chicken strips on a wire rack set over the sheet pan.

DAIRY-FREE TIP: Replace the whole milk with nondairy substitutes. Coconut or cashew milk would both work well in this recipe.

INGREDIENT TIP: Cornmeal is naturally gluten-free but is sometimes processed in plants where it can get cross-contaminated. Make sure yours is gluten-free. You also want the cornmeal to be finely ground so it'll cover the chicken tenders more easily. If you have only coarse cornmeal on hand, just pulse it in your food processor a couple of times.

Per serving Calories 188; Fat 6g; Total Carbohydrates 8g; Fiber 0g; Sodium 562mg; Protein 26g

BLACK BEAN and CHICKEN NACHOS

This recipe takes my Spicy Black Bean Nachos (page 67) and adds even more protein with shredded chicken! My husband and I make ourselves a pan of this for date nights. No need for plates, just let the baking dish cool, set it on the coffee table, and enjoy!

SERVES 4 / PREP TIME: 10 MINUTES / COOK TIME: 5 MINUTES

30-MINUTES

NUT-FREE

Nonstick cooking spray

5 cups corn tortilla chips

1 recipe Black Bean Dip (page 67)

1 cup shredded cooked chicken

1 cup shredded Monterey Jack cheese

¼ cup sliced jalapeño peppers

¼ cup sliced black olives

½ cup gluten-free salsa

1. Preheat the oven to 400°F. Lightly coat a 9-by-13-inch baking dish with cooking spray.

2. Spread out the tortilla chips in the bottom of the prepared baking dish. Spoon the black bean dip onto the chips, followed by the chicken. Scatter the cheese over the top, then finish with the jalapeño slices, black olives, and salsa.

3. Bake for 5 to 7 minutes, or until the cheese is melted. Serve hot.

DAIRY-FREE TIP: You can't have nachos without cheese, but nondairy cheese works just fine!

INGREDIENT TIP: Some store-bought salsas contain gluten. Check the label on yours to make sure it's gluten-free.

Per serving Calories 437; Fat 22g; Total Carbohydrates 37g; Fiber 8g; Sodium 1,036mg; Protein 25g

SLOW COOKER SHREDDED CHICKEN TACOS

This slow cooker shredded chicken is versatile and can be used in lots of different dishes. Use it as taco filling as in this recipe, put it on top of nachos, add it to your salads—the options are endless. I love to pop this in the slow cooker early on a Sunday and by evening I have delicious chicken I can use in a number of dishes during the week.

SERVES 6 / PREP TIME: 5 MINUTES / COOK TIME: 2 TO 6 HOURS

ONE-POT   5-INGREDIENTS

DAIRY-FREE

NUT-FREE

6 boneless, skinless
  chicken breasts

3 cups gluten-free salsa

¾ teaspoon red
  pepper flakes

¾ teaspoon garlic salt

12 corn tortillas, for serving

Taco toppings (optional),
  for serving

1. In a slow cooker, combine the chicken breasts, salsa, red pepper flakes, and garlic salt.

2. Cover and cook on high for 2 to 3 hours or on for low 4 to 6 hours.

3. Shred the chicken with two forks.

4. Serve on corn tortillas with your favorite toppings!

COOKING TIP: This recipe can be made in an Instant Pot as well.

INGREDIENT TIP: Some store-bought salsas contain gluten. Check the label on yours to make sure it's gluten-free.

Per serving Calories 307; Fat 4g; Total Carbohydrates 45g; Fiber 6g; Sodium 980mg; Protein 31g

EASY CHICKEN ENCHILADAS

Here's an easy way to use the chicken from the Slow Cooker Shredded Chicken Tacos (page 85)! For this recipe, you'll mix it with some delicious veggies and cream cheese to create creamy, protein-packed enchiladas that will keep your family happy and full! Serve with all your favorite enchilada toppings.

SERVES 6 / PREP TIME: 15 MINUTES / COOK TIME: 20 MINUTES

NUT-FREE

Nonstick cooking spray

6 cups shredded cooked chicken from Slow Cooker Shredded Chicken Tacos (page 85)

1 cup cream cheese, at room temperature

1 (4-ounce) can diced green chiles, drained

1 cup chopped scallion

½ cup chopped black olives

1 (28-ounce) can gluten-free enchilada sauce

10 to 14 corn tortillas

½ cup shredded Monterey Jack cheese

1. Preheat the oven to 400°F. Lightly coat a 9-by-13-inch baking dish with cooking spray.

2. In a large bowl, combine the chicken, cream cheese, chiles, scallion, and olives. Mix well.

3. Spread ½ cup of enchilada sauce in the bottom of the prepared baking dish.

4. Fill a corn tortilla with some of the chicken mixture, roll it up, and place it, seam-side down, in the baking dish. Repeat with the remaining tortillas and filling, lining up the enchiladas side by side so that they are touching.

5. Pour the remaining enchilada sauce over the enchiladas and sprinkle with the cheese.

6. Bake for 20 to 23 minutes, or until the cheese is bubbling.

7. Serve immediately.

DAIRY-FREE TIP: Replace the cream cheese and Monterey Jack with nondairy options.

INGREDIENT TIP: Store-bought sauces can contain gluten. Check the label on your enchilada sauce to make sure it's gluten-free.

Per serving Calories 562; Fat 24g; Total Carbohydrates 35g; Fiber 6g; Sodium 551mg; Protein 49g

BACON-WRAPPED CHICKEN with GOAT CHEESE

This is a fancy-looking dinner that takes only a couple minutes to prep. If you want to look like a professional chef with minimal work, this is the dish for you. I'm all for dishes that are simple and easy but look impressive.

SERVES 4 / PREP TIME: 15 MINUTES / COOK TIME: 25 MINUTES

ONE-PAN

NUT-FREE

4 boneless, skinless chicken breasts

½ teaspoon salt, divided

½ teaspoon freshly ground black pepper, divided

1 cup goat cheese

¼ cup chopped scallions

4 slices bacon

1 tablespoon olive oil

2 tablespoons unsalted butter

1 tablespoon all-purpose gluten-free flour blend

1 cup gluten-free chicken broth

2 tablespoons gluten-free Dijon mustard

½ cup whole milk

1. Butterfly the chicken breasts by cutting each breast in half horizontally but not all the way through and then opening it like a book. Place each chicken breast between two sheets of plastic wrap and gently pound it thin. Season the butterflied chicken breasts with ¼ teaspoon of salt and ¼ teaspoon of pepper.

2. Divide the goat cheese and scallions among the butterflied chicken breasts and roll them up. Wrap a slice of bacon around each roll and secure with a toothpick.

3. In a pan, heat the olive oil over medium-high heat. Cook the bacon-wrapped chicken until brown on all sides, 5 to 8 minutes. Transfer the chicken to a plate.

4. In the same pan, melt the butter and whisk in the flour blend. Cook for 1 minute before whisking in the chicken broth, mustard, milk, and remaining ¼ teaspoon of salt and ¼ teaspoon of pepper.

5. Return the chicken to the pan, cover, reduce the heat to low, and cook for 15 to 17 more minutes, or until the chicken is cooked through and no longer pink. Serve immediately.

TIP: Gluten is present in many store-bought stocks and condiments. Check the labels to make sure your chicken broth and mustard are gluten-free.

Per serving Calories 416; Fat 26g; Total Carbohydrates 5g; Fiber 1g; Sodium 1,367mg; Protein 40g

SPICY TURKEY-STUFFED BELL PEPPERS

These bell peppers are stuffed with a spicy filling packed with protein. They taste so hearty you'd never guess they're also healthy for you! Vegetables, protein, healthy carbs—who knew a bell pepper could hold an entire balanced meal?

SERVES 4 / PREP TIME: 10 MINUTES / COOK TIME: 45 MINUTES

DAIRY-FREE

NUT-FREE

8 red or green bell peppers

2 cups water

1 cup quinoa

1 tablespoon olive oil

1 pound ground turkey

½ cup chopped onion

1 (15-ounce) can diced tomatoes, drained

3 tablespoons Homemade Taco Seasoning (page 126)

¼ teaspoon salt

¼ teaspoon freshly ground black pepper

1. Preheat the oven to 375°F.

2. Slice off the top of each bell pepper and spoon out the seeds and ribs. If necessary, cut a thin slice off the bottom of each pepper to allow them to sit upright.

3. Stand the peppers on a rimmed sheet pan, cover with aluminum foil, and bake for 12 minutes.

4. While the peppers bake, in a small saucepan, bring the water to a boil over medium-high heat. Stir in the quinoa and olive oil. Reduce the heat, cover, and simmer for 12 to 15 minutes, or until the quinoa is cooked.

5. In a large pan, cook the turkey and onion over medium heat until the turkey is brown, about 4 minutes.

6. Stir in the diced tomatoes, taco seasoning, salt, and pepper. Simmer for 2 to 3 minutes, then remove from the heat.

7. Stir the quinoa into the turkey mixture.

8. Fill the peppers with the quinoa-turkey mixture.

9. Stand the stuffed peppers back on the sheet pan and cover it with aluminum foil. Bake for 15 to 18 minutes, or until the stuffing is heated through. Serve immediately.

Per serving Calories 475; Fat 17g; Total Carbohydrates 55g; Fiber 9g; Sodium 553mg; Protein 30g

TEX-MEX TURKEY QUINOA

My family raves about this one-pan dinner—and so do I. I love it for how quick it is: Just throw everything in a pan, and in 25 minutes, dinner is ready. And don't tell your kids, but between the lean turkey, the protein-rich quinoa, and all the nutrients in the sweet potato, it's really pretty good for them!

SERVES 4 / PREP TIME: 10 MINUTES / COOK TIME: 30 MINUTES

ONE-PAN

NUT-FREE

1 pound ground turkey

1 (19-ounce) can gluten-free enchilada sauce

1 (15-ounce) can black beans, drained and rinsed

1 small sweet potato, well scrubbed and chopped

1 cup quinoa

1 cup water

1 (4-ounce) can roasted green chiles, drained

2 tablespoons Homemade Taco Seasoning (page 126)

¼ teaspoon salt

¼ teaspoon freshly ground black pepper

½ cup shredded Monterey Jack cheese

1. In a large pan, brown the turkey over medium heat for about 4 minutes. Drain off any grease from the pan.

2. Stir in the enchilada sauce, black beans, sweet potato, quinoa, water, chiles, taco seasoning, salt, and pepper.

3. Cover the pan and reduce the heat to medium-low. Cook for 20 to 25 minutes, or until the quinoa is fully cooked and tender.

4. Sprinkle the cheese over the quinoa, then cover again and cook for 2 minutes, or until the cheese melts. Serve immediately.

DAIRY-FREE TIP: Replace the cheese with a nondairy substitute, or omit it entirely.

INGREDIENT TIP: Store-bought sauces can contain gluten. Check the label to make sure your enchilada sauce is gluten-free.

Per serving Calories 474; Fat 17g; Total Carbohydrates 46g; Fiber 9g; Sodium 771mg; Protein 34g

Cheesy Italian Meatballs (page 103)

CHAPTER SEVEN

Beef and Pork Main Dishes

EASY SALISBURY STEAK

I didn't grow up eating Salisbury steak, but I wish I had! I didn't know what I was missing out on all those years. Serve it on top of some Creamy Mashed Potatoes (page 39) with a side of green beans to make your soul (and your taste buds) happy. It's total comfort goodness made in one pan—a winner of a dinner.

SERVES 4 / PREP TIME: 10 MINUTES / COOK TIME: 15 MINUTES

ONE-PAN   30-MINUTES

NUT-FREE

1 pound lean ground beef

⅓ cup gluten-free cornmeal

4 tablespoons gluten-free ketchup, divided

1 tablespoon gluten-free mustard

½ teaspoon garlic powder

½ teaspoon onion powder

½ teaspoon salt, divided

½ teaspoon freshly ground black pepper, divided

1 tablespoon olive oil

2 cups gluten-free beef broth

4 tablespoons (½ stick) unsalted butter, melted

¼ cup all-purpose gluten-free flour blend

Chopped fresh parsley, for garnish

1. In a medium bowl, combine the ground beef, cornmeal, 2 tablespoons of ketchup, mustard, garlic powder, onion powder, ¼ teaspoon of salt, and ¼ teaspoon of pepper. Divide the mixture into 4 equal portions and shape each into a patty.

2. In a large pan, heat the olive oil over medium heat. Cook the patties on both sides for 8 to 10 minutes, or until they're no longer pink. Reduce the heat to low.

3. In a small bowl, whisk together the beef broth, butter, flour blend, remaining 2 tablespoons of ketchup, remaining ¼ teaspoon of salt, and remaining ¼ teaspoon of pepper. Pour the mixture into the pan around the patties.

4. Simmer, whisking occasionally, for 1 to 2 minutes, or until the gravy thickens.

5. Garnish with fresh parsley and serve.

DAIRY-FREE TIP: Replace the butter with a nondairy substitute.

INGREDIENT TIP: Store-bought broths and condiments can contain gluten, and although cornmeal is naturally gluten-free, it's sometimes processed in plants where it can be cross-contaminated. Check the labels on your cornmeal, ketchup, mustard, and beef broth to make sure they're gluten-free.

Per serving Calories 385; Fat 22g; Total Carbohydrates 19g; Fiber 2g; Sodium 1,010mg; Protein 29g

QUESADILLA CASSEROLE

Make this for a main course or a delicious side dish to bring to a potluck. You can't go wrong with all those delicious taco flavors packed into a cheesy, beefy rice casserole.

SERVES 6 / PREP TIME: 10 MINUTES / COOK TIME: 35 MINUTES

NUT-FREE

Nonstick cooking spray

1 pound lean ground beef

1 medium white onion, chopped

2 tablespoons minced garlic

3 cups cooked rice

1 (15-ounce) can black beans, drained and rinsed

2 cups gluten-free enchilada sauce

1 cup Best Taco Sauce Ever (page 127)

½ cup canned or frozen corn kernels

3 tablespoons Homemade Taco Seasoning (page 126)

½ cup shredded Cheddar cheese

1. Preheat the oven to 350°F. Coat a 9-by-13-inch baking dish with cooking spray.

2. In a large pan, cook the beef, onion, and garlic over medium-high heat for 7 to 10 minutes, or until the beef is browned. Drain off any grease.

3. Transfer the cooked beef mixture to the prepared baking dish. Add the cooked rice, black beans, enchilada sauce, taco sauce, corn kernels, and taco seasoning. Stir everything together.

4. Cover with aluminum foil and bake for 20 minutes.

5. Remove the foil and sprinkle the cheese all over the casserole. Bake for an additional 5 minutes, or until the cheese is melted. Serve immediately.

DAIRY-FREE TIP: Replace the cheese with a nondairy alternative, or omit it entirely.

INGREDIENT TIP: Store-bought sauces can contain gluten. Check the labels to make sure your enchilada sauce (and taco sauce if you use store-bought) is gluten-free.

Per serving Calories 342; Fat 14g; Total Carbohydrates 32g; Fiber 5g; Sodium 998mg; Protein 22g

BEEF CHILI

My lazy beef chili gets raves every time I make it. The secret ingredient is your favorite brand of sweet and smoky dry rub, which adds a ton of delicious flavor for very little effort. You can make this chili quickly in an Instant Pot or slowly in a slow cooker. Either way, it's a super convenient way to keep your family happy and full.

SERVES 6 / PREP TIME: 10 MINUTES / COOK TIME: 20 MINUTES OR 2 TO 6 HOURS

DAIRY-FREE

NUT-FREE

Nonstick cooking spray

1 pound lean ground beef

1 small onion, chopped

2 (24-ounce) cans diced tomatoes

2 (15-ounce) cans red beans, drained and rinsed

4 to 5 tablespoons sweet and smoky dry rub

2 tablespoons garlic powder

½ teaspoon salt

¼ teaspoon freshly ground black pepper

IN AN INSTANT POT

1. Press the Sauté button. Lightly coat the pot with cooking spray. Add the ground beef and brown it. Drain off any grease.

2. Add the onion, tomatoes with their juice, red beans, dry rub, garlic powder, salt, and pepper.

3. Close the lid and pressure-cook at High Pressure for 10 minutes with natural release.

IN A SLOW COOKER

1. In a large pan, cook the ground beef over medium-high heat for 7 to 10 minutes, or until it's browned. Drain off any grease.

2. Transfer the cooked ground beef to a slow cooker. Add the onion, tomatoes with their juice, red beans, dry rub, garlic powder, salt, and pepper. Mix well.

3. Cover and cook on low for 5 to 6 hours or on high for 2 to 3 hours.

INGREDIENT TIP: Store-bought seasonings are usually, but not always, gluten-free. Check the label to make sure your dry rub is gluten-free.

Per serving Calories 275; Fat 10g; Total Carbohydrates 26g; Fiber 10g; Sodium 470mg; Protein 23g

ONE-POT HAMBURGER-PASTA DINNER

This recipe is my healthier, homemade version of those quick Hamburger Helper–style dinners. Instead of a box of processed ingredients that may contain gluten, this recipe uses natural, clean ingredients—but it's still easy to whip up, and it still has major comfort-food vibes. I like to serve it with Quick Pickled Onions (page 132).

SERVES 6 / PREP TIME: 10 MINUTES / COOK TIME: 15 MINUTES

ONE-PAN   30-MINUTES

NUT-FREE

2 tablespoons olive oil

1 pound lean ground beef

1 medium onion, chopped

2 tablespoons minced garlic

4 cups cooked gluten-free elbow macaroni

1 (15-ounce) can diced tomatoes

1 (8-ounce) can gluten-free tomato paste

½ cup shredded Cheddar cheese

¼ cup gluten-free yellow mustard

½ teaspoon salt

¼ teaspoon freshly ground black pepper

1. In a large pan, heat the olive oil over medium-high heat. Add the beef, onion, and garlic and cook for 7 to 10 minutes, or until the beef is browned. Drain off any grease.

2. Add the cooked pasta, diced tomatoes with their juice, and tomato paste and cook for 5 to 8 minutes, or until everything is thoroughly mixed and heated through.

3. Stir in the cheese, mustard, salt, and pepper. Serve immediately.

DAIRY-FREE TIP: Replace the Cheddar cheese with a nondairy substitute.

INGREDIENT TIP: Store-bought condiments can contain gluten, and store-bought tomato paste is usually, but not always, gluten-free. Check the labels on your mustard and tomato paste to make sure they're gluten-free.

Per serving Calories 534; Fat 19g; Total Carbohydrates 73g; Fiber 6g; Sodium 462mg; Protein 24g

EASY BEEF STROGANOFF

This is the beef stroganoff I grew up on. Later in life, I realized it's not exactly a traditional beef stroganoff recipe, but I still make it because it tastes delicious, and it's relatively easy to make with gluten-free ingredients. Plus it's so easy to pull together! I love any recipe that doesn't require anything fancy to produce a hearty, tasty dinner.

SERVES 4 / PREP TIME: 5 MINUTES / COOK TIME: 20 MINUTES

ONE-PAN   30-MINUTES

NUT-FREE

½ teaspoon olive oil

1 small onion, chopped

1 pound lean ground beef

1 (16-ounce) can gluten-free tomato soup

2 tablespoons gluten-free Worcestershire sauce (optional)

½ cup sour cream

4 cups cooked rice

1. In a large pan, heat the olive oil over medium heat. Add the onion and sauté until translucent, about 4 minutes.

2. Add the ground beef, raise the heat to medium-high, and cook for 7 to 10 minutes, or until the beef is browned. Drain off any grease.

3. Turn the heat back down to medium, stir in the tomato soup and Worcestershire (if using), and cook for 6 to 8 minutes, or until the soup is warmed through.

4. Reduce the heat to a simmer and gradually stir in the sour cream.

5. Serve over a bed of rice.

INGREDIENT TIP: Many store-bought soups and sauces contain gluten. Check the labels on your tomato soup and Worcestershire sauce (if using) to make sure they're gluten-free.

Per serving Calories 689; Fat 22g; Total Carbohydrates 92g; Fiber 3g; Sodium 720mg; Protein 32g

VEGGIE-PACKED MEATLOAF

You may not think of meatloaf as health food, but when you see how many veggies are packed into this one, you might change your mind. Serve it with some classic meatloaf side dishes like Creamy Mashed Potatoes (page 39) and Sweet Butter-Roasted Carrots (page 43).

SERVES 6 / PREP TIME: 10 MINUTES / COOK TIME: 1 HOUR

NUT-FREE

Nonstick cooking spray

1 teaspoon olive oil

1 cup diced onion

1 cup finely diced carrot

½ cup diced green
  bell pepper

1 teaspoon minced garlic

1 pound lean ground beef

1 cup gluten-free cornmeal

2 large eggs, lightly beaten

¼ cup gluten-free ketchup,
  plus 3 tablespoons,
  divided

¼ cup whole milk

1. Preheat the oven to 400°F. Lightly coat an 8½-by-4½-inch loaf pan with cooking spray.

2. In a small pan, heat the olive oil over medium heat. Add the onion, carrot, bell pepper, and garlic and sauté for 5 to 8 minutes, or until the vegetables are tender.

3. Transfer the cooked veggies to a mixing bowl and add the ground beef, cornmeal, eggs, ¼ cup of ketchup, and milk. Mix well to combine.

4. Spoon the mixture into the prepared loaf pan and bake for 40 to 45 minutes, or until the internal temperature of the loaf reaches 155°F.

5. Spoon the remaining 3 tablespoons of ketchup over the top of the loaf and bake for an additional 10 minutes.

6. Let the meatloaf sit for 10 minutes before serving.

INGREDIENT TIP: Store-bought condiments can contain gluten, and although cornmeal is naturally gluten-free, it may be processed in a plant where it can be cross-contaminated. Check the labels on your ketchup and cornmeal to make sure they're gluten-free.

Per serving Calories 285; Fat 13g; Total Carbohydrates 25g; Fiber 2g; Sodium 315mg; Protein 20g

BEEF and BROCCOLI

I dearly missed Chinese food after receiving my diagnosis and knew I needed to find a way to re-create some Chinese takeout dishes at home. This dish, served over a bed of rice or quinoa, is the perfect solution. It uses just a few simple ingredients but achieves great results. Serve over rice or quinoa.

SERVES 6 / PREP TIME: 10 MINUTES / COOK TIME: 25 MINUTES OR 2 TO 4 HOURS

DAIRY-FREE

NUT-FREE

Nonstick cooking spray

1 pound beef round steak

1 teaspoon salt

1 teaspoon freshly ground black pepper

2 cups gluten-free beef broth

½ cup gluten-free soy sauce

½ cup brown sugar

2 tablespoons minced garlic

3 tablespoons gluten-free cornstarch

4 cups chopped broccoli florets

IN AN INSTANT POT

1. Press the Sauté button. Lightly coat the pot with cooking spray. Season the beef with the salt and pepper. Sear the beef for 1 to 2 minutes per side, to lock in the juices.

2. Add the broth, soy sauce, brown sugar, and garlic.

3. Close the lid and pressure-cook at High Pressure for 11 minutes with rapid release. Carefully open the lid.

4. Let the beef cool on a cutting board for 5 to 8 minutes, or until it's cool enough to handle. Cut the beef into thin strips.

5. Meanwhile, pour ½ cup of the liquid from the Instant Pot into a small bowl and whisk in the cornstarch. Slowly pour the mixture into the Instant Pot, whisking constantly.

6. Return the beef strips back to the Instant Pot and add the broccoli florets.

7. Close the lid and cook at Low Pressure for 5 minutes with rapid release.

IN A SLOW COOKER

1. Season the beef with the salt and pepper, then cut it into thin strips.

2. Put the beef strips in a slow cooker. Add the broth, soy sauce, brown sugar, and garlic.

3. Cover and cook on high for 1 to 2 hours or on low for 2 to 3 hours.

4. Pour ½ cup of the liquid from the slow cooker into a small bowl and whisk in the cornstarch. Slowly pour the mixture into the slow cooker, whisking constantly.

5. Add the broccoli. Cook on high for an additional 1 hour, or until the broccoli is tender when pierced with a fork.

INGREDIENT TIP: Store-bought condiments and broths can contain gluten, and although cornstarch is naturally gluten-free, it's sometimes processed in plants where it can be cross-contaminated. Check the labels on your beef broth, soy sauce, and cornstarch to make sure they're gluten-free.

Per serving Calories 273; Fat 7g; Total Carbohydrates 23g; Fiber 2g; Sodium 1,910mg; Protein 29g

SHEET-PAN BEEF FAJITAS

A no-fuss recipe with easy cleanup? Yes, please! Just throw everything on a sheet pan and bake. Serve the fajitas with corn tortillas and whatever toppings you like, such as guacamole, sour cream, salsa—just make sure any store-bought items are gluten-free.

SERVES 8 / PREP TIME: 10 MINUTES / COOK TIME: 25 MINUTES

SHEET PAN

DAIRY-FREE

NUT-FREE

Nonstick cooking spray

3 tablespoons gluten-free fajita seasoning

2 tablespoons olive oil

2 tablespoons water

1 pound skirt steak, thinly sliced

1 red bell pepper, seeded and thinly sliced

1 green bell pepper, seeded and thinly sliced

1 red onion, thinly sliced

½ teaspoon salt

½ teaspoon freshly ground black pepper

10 to 12 corn tortillas

1. Preheat the oven to 375°F. Line a rimmed sheet pan with aluminum foil and lightly coat the foil with cooking spray.

2. In a small bowl, whisk together the fajita seasoning, olive oil, and water.

3. Spread out the sliced beef, bell peppers, and onion in a single layer on the prepared sheet pan.

4. Drizzle the fajita seasoning mixture over the beef and veggies. Season with the salt and pepper.

5. Bake for 20 to 25 minutes, or until the beef is cooked through and the veggies are tender.

6. Serve with the corn tortillas.

INGREDIENT TIP: Store-bought seasoning packets are usually, but not always, gluten-free. Check the label to make sure your fajita seasoning is gluten-free, or use the recipe for Homemade Taco Seasoning (page 126).

Per serving Calories 288; Fat 11g; Total Carbohydrates 33g; Fiber 5g; Sodium 361mg; Protein 15g

CHUNKY BEEF STEW

This thick, chunky stew is packed with beef, potatoes, and vegetables. Hello, comfort food on a cold winter night!

SERVES 6 / PREP TIME: 10 MINUTES / COOK TIME: 25 MINUTES

DAIRY-FREE

NUT-FREE

2 tablespoons olive oil

1 pound sirloin steak, cut into ½-inch cubes

3 cups chopped peeled potatoes

4 medium carrots, peeled and sliced

4 celery stalks, sliced

1 small onion, chopped

4 cups gluten-free beef broth

2 tablespoons minced garlic

1 teaspoon dried rosemary

½ teaspoon dried thyme

1 teaspoon salt

½ teaspoon freshly ground black pepper

3 tablespoons gluten-free cornstarch

1. In a large saucepan, heat the olive oil over medium-high heat. Add the steak, potatoes, carrots, celery, and onion and cook for 7 to 10 minutes, or until the beef is browned.

2. Add the broth, garlic, rosemary, thyme, salt, and pepper. Bring to a boil, then reduce the heat, cover, and simmer for 14 minutes.

3. Transfer ¼ cup of the liquid from the pot to a small bowl. Whisk in the cornstarch.

4. Slowly pour the cornstarch mixture into the stew, whisking constantly.

5. Bring the stew back to a boil and cook for 2 minutes. Serve.

INGREDIENT TIP: Store-bought broths can contain gluten, and although cornstarch is naturally gluten-free, it's sometimes processed in plants where it can be cross-contaminated. Check the labels to make sure your beef broth and cornstarch are gluten-free.

Per serving Calories 277; Fat 9g; Total Carbohydrates 26g; Fiber 4g; Sodium 941mg; Protein 23g

CREAMY MUSHROOM and HAM PASTA

Sometimes even I'm surprised by just how quickly this recipe comes together. It's ready in just 20 minutes! Before you know it, you'll have a thick, creamy mushroom and ham sauce slathered over your favorite gluten-free pasta.

SERVES 4 / PREP TIME: 10 MINUTES / COOK TIME: 10 MINUTES

ONE-POT   30-MINUTES

NUT-FREE

2 tablespoons olive oil

1 cup chopped mushrooms

1 tablespoon minced garlic

1 teaspoon dried parsley

1 teaspoon dried oregano

½ teaspoon salt

1 cup chopped ham

1 cup whole milk

1 tablespoon all-purpose gluten-free flour blend

3 cups cooked gluten-free penne pasta

1. In a large pan, heat the olive oil over medium heat. Add the mushrooms, garlic, parsley, oregano, and salt and sauté for about 5 minutes, or until the mushrooms are tender and fragrant.

2. Add the ham, milk, and flour blend and stir constantly until the sauce thickens, about 5 minutes.

3. Pour over the pasta and serve.

DAIRY-FREE TIP: Swap out the milk for a nondairy option like coconut milk.

Per serving Calories 317; Fat 12g; Total Carbohydrates 41g; Fiber 3g; Sodium 747mg; Protein 11g

CHEESY ITALIAN MEATBALLS

Make these meatballs for your next Italian night! In fact, why not double the recipe and freeze some for the Italian night after that? All you have to do is whip everything together in a bowl, stuff the mozzarella into the center, and bake. No need for store-bought frozen meatballs with processed ingredients and hidden gluten ever again. Serve these with your favorite gluten-free pasta and marinara sauce.

SERVES 4 / PREP TIME: 10 MINUTES / COOK TIME: 20 MINUTES

SHEET PAN **5-INGREDIENTS** **30-MINUTES**

NUT-FREE

Nonstick cooking spray

1 pound ground gluten-free Italian sausage

¼ cup gluten-free cornmeal

1 large egg, lightly beaten

1 teaspoon garlic powder

½ teaspoon salt

½ teaspoon freshly ground black pepper

2 ounces mozzarella cheese, cut into 20 cubes

2 tablespoons chopped basil, for garnish

3 tablespoons shaved Parmesan, for garnish

1. Preheat the oven to 350°F. Line a rimmed sheet pan with aluminum foil and lightly coat the foil with cooking spray.

2. In a large bowl, combine the sausage, cornmeal, egg, garlic powder, salt, and pepper.

3. Form a meatball around each small cube of mozzarella. You should get about 20 meatballs.

4. Put the meatballs on the prepared sheet pan and bake for 15 to 20 minutes, or until the centers are no longer pink. Serve immediately, garnished with the basil and Parmesan.

INGREDIENT TIP: Cornmeal is naturally gluten-free but is sometimes processed in a plant where it can be cross-contaminated. Store-bought sausage sometimes has gluten hiding in it, too. Check the label to make sure your cornmeal and sausage are gluten-free.

Per serving Calories 565; Fat 45g; Total Carbohydrates 9g; Fiber 1g; Sodium 1,485mg; Protein 29g

ITALIAN STUFFED-PEPPER "PIZZAS"

These bell pepper "pizzas" give you all the delicious flavors of pizza, but without all the carbs. Just fill the bell peppers with meat, cheese, and your favorite pizza toppings, and in under 30 minutes, you have a tasty, healthy alternative to pizza!

SERVES 8 / PREP TIME: 10 MINUTES / COOK TIME: 25 MINUTES

SHEET PAN **5-INGREDIENTS**

NUT-FREE

4 bell peppers, halved lengthwise and seeded

1 pound ground gluten-free Italian sausage

1 (15-ounce) jar gluten-free pizza sauce

Optional toppings: Chopped onion, chopped green olives, chopped gluten-free pepperoni, etc.

1 cup shredded mozzarella cheese

1. Preheat the oven to 375°F.

2. Place the bell pepper halves on a rimmed sheet pan. Bake for 8 to 10 minutes.

3. Meanwhile, in a large pan, brown the Italian sausage over medium heat. Drain off any grease.

4. Fill each pepper half with ¼ cup pizza sauce. Fill each with some of the Italian sausage and any other toppings you'd like.

5. Sprinkle with the cheese. Bake for 13 to 16 minutes, or until the cheese is melted.

DAIRY-FREE TIP: Use a nondairy cheese alternative.

INGREDIENT TIP: Gluten is sometimes present in store-bought sauces and sausages. Check the labels to make sure your pizza sauce and Italian sausage are gluten-free.

Per serving Calories 417; Fat 31g; Total Carbohydrates 14g; Fiber 2g; Sodium 1,627mg; Protein 23g

CHEESY PIZZA PASTA CASSEROLE

This is one of my favorite recipes, with all those pizza flavors wrapped up in a cheesy pasta casserole. I've included my favorite pizza toppings—mushrooms, olives, and pepperoni, but you can easily switch them out for bell peppers, sausage, bacon, or whatever else fits your family!

SERVES 8 / PREP TIME: 10 MINUTES / COOK TIME: 30 MINUTES

NUT-FREE

Nonstick cooking spray

1 teaspoon olive oil

1 small onion, chopped

2 tablespoons minced garlic

5 cups cooked gluten-free penne pasta

2½ cups gluten-free pizza sauce

2 cups chopped mushrooms

1 cup chopped gluten-free pepperoni

½ cup chopped black olives

½ cup shredded mozzarella cheese

½ cup grated Parmesan cheese

1. Preheat the oven to 350°F. Lightly coat a 9-by-13-inch baking dish with cooking spray.

2. In a large saucepan, heat the olive oil over medium heat. Add the onion and garlic and sauté for 3 minutes.

3. Stir in the cooked pasta, pizza sauce, mushrooms, pepperoni, black olives, and mozzarella.

4. Pour the contents of the pan into the prepared baking dish. Top with the Parmesan cheese.

5. Bake for 20 to 25 minutes, or until the dish is bubbly. Serve immediately.

INGREDIENT TIP: Store-bought sauces and sausages can contain gluten. Check the labels on your pizza sauce and pepperoni to make sure they're gluten-free.

Per serving Calories 437; Fat 17g; Total Carbohydrates 60g; Fiber 1g; Sodium 684mg; Protein 13g

BASIL-GARLIC PORK CHOPS and POTATOES

It takes just a few simple, fresh ingredients to elevate pork chops to a full meal. I particularly love this dish during the summer, when my herb garden is exploding with all the basil my heart desires, but pork chops and potatoes will hit the spot on a chilly autumn night as well.

SERVES 4 / PREP TIME: 10 MINUTES, PLUS 15 MINUTES TO MARINATE / COOK TIME: 35 MINUTES

SHEET PAN

DAIRY-FREE

NUT-FREE

Nonstick cooking spray

1 cup finely chopped fresh basil leaves

3 tablespoons freshly squeezed lemon juice

4 tablespoons olive oil, divided

2 tablespoons minced garlic

4 (¾-inch-thick) bone-in pork chops

1 teaspoon salt

½ teaspoon freshly ground black pepper

4 red potatoes, quartered

1. Preheat the oven to 350°F. Line a rimmed sheet pan with aluminum foil and lightly coat the foil with cooking spray.

2. In a shallow baking dish, whisk together the basil, lemon juice, 3 tablespoons of olive oil, and the garlic. Put the pork chops in the dish and coat them well with the marinade. Set aside to marinate for 15 minutes.

3. Put the potatoes on one half of the prepared sheet pan and drizzle them with the remaining 1 tablespoon of olive oil.

4. Put the pork chops on the other half of the sheet pan and drizzle the marinade over both the pork chops and the potatoes. Sprinkle both with the salt and pepper.

5. Bake for 30 to 35 minutes, or until the internal temperature of the pork chops reaches 145°F. Serve immediately.

Per serving Calories 622; Fat 36g; Total Carbohydrates 38g; Fiber 4g; Sodium 598mg; Protein 37g

HONEY-MUSTARD PORK CHOPS and GREEN BEANS

This recipe makes for a quick, easy, and delicious weeknight meal. Slathered with a homemade honey-mustard sauce alongside roasted green beans, these pork chops are sure to delight.

SERVES 4 / PREP TIME: 5 MINUTES / COOK TIME: 15 MINUTES

ONE-PAN   30-MINUTES

DAIRY-FREE

NUT-FREE

¼ cup honey

3 tablespoons gluten-free yellow mustard

½ teaspoon garlic powder

2 tablespoons olive oil

4 (¾-inch-thick) bone-in pork chops

3 cups cut green beans

½ teaspoon salt

½ teaspoon freshly ground black pepper

1. In a small bowl, whisk together the honey, mustard, and garlic powder.

2. In a large pan, heat the olive oil over medium heat. Sear the pork chops on both sides for 1 to 2 minutes, or until browned.

3. Brush the honey-mustard sauce over the pork chops, then turn the chops over and brush the flip side with the remaining sauce.

4. Arrange the green beans around the pork chops and season with the salt and pepper.

5. Cover and reduce the heat to low. Cook for 10 to 15 minutes, or until the green beans are tender and the pork chops are no longer pink inside.

INGREDIENT TIP: Store-bought condiments can contain gluten. Check the label on your mustard to make sure it's gluten-free.

Per serving Calories 502; Fat 31g; Total Carbohydrates 26g; Fiber 3g; Sodium 430mg; Protein 35g

Classic Chocolate Chip Oatmeal Cookies (page 111)

Desserts and Sweet Treats

EDIBLE COOKIE DOUGH

I heart cookie dough, but it usually has both gluten and raw eggs in it—unsafe to eat on two counts! This version is not only gluten-free and dairy-free but also free of raw eggs. And by quickly cooking the flour in the microwave before you get started, you've taken all the necessary steps to eat raw edible cookie dough with peace of mind! Hand me a spoon and a glass of wine, please and thank you.

SERVES 6 / PREP TIME: 10 MINUTES

30-MINUTES

NUT-FREE

VEGETARIAN

1 cup all-purpose gluten-free flour blend

8 tablespoons (1 stick) unsalted butter

1 cup confectioners' sugar

¼ cup brown sugar

3 tablespoons whole milk

1 teaspoon vanilla extract

½ teaspoon sea salt

½ cup mini chocolate chips

1. Put the flour blend in a small microwavable bowl and microwave on high for 1 minute. Allow the flour to cool.

2. Transfer the flour blend to a medium bowl and add the butter, confectioners' sugar, brown sugar, milk, vanilla extract, and sea salt. Mix well to combine. Fold in the chocolate chips.

3. Store in an airtight container. Eat cold or at room temperature.

DAIRY-FREE TIP: Swap out the milk and butter for nondairy alternatives.

Per serving Calories 330; Fat 20g; Total Carbohydrates 34g; Fiber 3g; Sodium 281mg; Protein 4g

CLASSIC CHOCOLATE CHIP OATMEAL COOKIES

For a long time, I wasn't a fan of oatmeal cookies, because they always seemed to contain raisins. But once I realized you could just use chocolate chips instead, I was instantly hooked. This recipe is perfect for the cookie lover who can't have gluten and prefers chocolate chips to raisins.

MAKES 18 COOKIES / PREP TIME: 10 MINUTES / COOK TIME: 10 MINUTES

SHEET PAN   30-MINUTES

NUT-FREE

VEGETARIAN

8 tablespoons (1 stick) unsalted butter, at room temperature

½ cup granulated sugar

½ cup brown sugar

2 large eggs

½ teaspoon vanilla extract

1 teaspoon ground cinnamon

½ teaspoon salt

½ teaspoon baking soda

⅔ cup all-purpose gluten-free flour blend

3 cups gluten-free certified rolled oats

¼ cup chocolate chips

1. Preheat the oven to 350°F. Line two rimmed sheet pans with parchment paper.

2. In a medium bowl, beat together the butter and sugars. Add the eggs, one at a time, and cream together.

3. Stir in the vanilla extract, cinnamon, salt, and baking soda, then gradually add the flour blend. Mix well.

4. Fold in the oats and chocolate chips.

5. Drop spoonfuls of the dough onto the prepared sheet pans about 2 inches apart.

6. Bake for 10 to 12 minutes, or until the edges are nicely browned.

7. Allow the cookies to cool on the sheet pans for at least 5 minutes before transferring them to a wire rack to cool completely.

DAIRY-FREE TIP: Replace the butter with a nondairy alternative.

VEGAN TIP: Swap out the eggs for a vegan egg-replacement option.

(1 cookie) Calories 188; Fat 8g; Total Carbohydrates 26g; Fiber 2g; Sodium 148mg; Protein 3g

CHEWY CHOCOLATE CHIP COOKIES

Chewy and crispy at the edges, soft on the inside—is that not the perfect chocolate chip cookie? That's what makes this recipe one of my absolute favorites for any occasion—even those spur-of-the-moment late-night cravings, because it's so quick and easy to make.

MAKES 18 COOKIES / PREP TIME: 10 MINUTES / COOK TIME: 10 MINUTES

SHEET PAN   30-MINUTES

NUT-FREE

VEGETARIAN

8 tablespoons (1 stick) unsalted butter, at room temperature

½ cup granulated sugar

½ cup brown sugar

2 large eggs

½ teaspoon vanilla extract

½ teaspoon salt

½ teaspoon baking soda

1¼ cups all-purpose gluten-free flour blend

½ cup chocolate chips

1. Preheat the oven to 350°F. Line two rimmed sheet pans with parchment paper.

2. In a medium bowl, beat together the butter and sugars. Add the, eggs one at a time, and cream together.

3. Stir in the vanilla extract, salt, and baking soda, then gradually add the flour blend. Mix well.

4. Fold in the chocolate chips.

5. Drop spoonfuls of the dough onto the prepared sheet pans about 2 inches apart.

6. Bake for 9 to 11 minutes, or until the edges are nicely browned.

7. Allow the cookies to cool on the sheet pans for at least 5 minutes before transferring them to a wire rack to cool completely.

DAIRY-FREE TIP: Swap out the butter for a nondairy alternative.

(1 cookie) Calories 185; Fat 8g; Total Carbohydrates 27g; Fiber 2g; Sodium 147mg; Protein 3g

FLOURLESS DOUBLE CHOCOLATE CHIP COOKIES

You might be skeptical as you whip together the batter for these cookies, but trust me—you *can* have cookies without flour! People will be in awe once they find out what's actually in these chewy treats.

MAKES 18 COOKIES / PREP TIME: 10 MINUTES / COOK TIME: 15 MINUTES

SHEET PAN   30-MINUTES

DAIRY-FREE

NUT-FREE

VEGETARIAN

2 ½ cups confectioners' sugar

½ cup unsweetened cocoa powder

¼ teaspoon ground cinnamon

½ teaspoon salt

3 large egg whites

1 teaspoon vanilla extract

2 ½ cups semisweet chocolate chips

1. Preheat the oven to 350°F. Line two rimmed sheet pans with parchment paper.

2. In a bowl, whisk together the confectioners' sugar, cocoa powder, cinnamon, and salt.

3. Stir in the egg whites and vanilla extract.

4. Fold in the chocolate chips.

5. Drop tablespoons of batter onto the prepared sheet pans about 2 inches apart.

6. Bake for 15 to 17 minutes, or until the cookies start cracking on the surface.

7. Allow the cookies to cool on the sheet pans for 10 minutes before carefully transferring them to a wire rack to cool completely.

(1 cookie) Calories 181; Fat 9g; Total Carbohydrates 26g; Fiber 1g; Sodium 72mg; Protein 3g

FLOURLESS DOUBLE-CHOCOLATE CAKE

Anytime I'm in a restaurant with a flourless chocolate cake on the menu, I'm on cloud nine. I absolutely love the thick, dense, intense chocolate flavor you find in flourless chocolate cakes. This recipe is safe because no flour means no gluten—but dangerous because you can now make this decadent treat at home anytime you want. Serve with fresh fruit or fresh whipped cream.

SERVES 8 / PREP TIME: 15 MINUTES / COOK TIME: 40 MINUTES

NUT-FREE

VEGETARIAN

Nonstick cooking spray

6 large eggs

⅓ cup sugar

1½ cups chocolate chips

1 cup (2 sticks) unsalted butter

1 tablespoon vanilla extract

1 teaspoon salt

⅓ cup unsweetened cocoa powder

1. Preheat the oven to 450°F. Put on a kettle of water to boil. Line the bottom of an 8-inch springform pan with a circle of parchment paper. Spray the parchment circle and walls of the pan with cooking spray. Wrap the outside of the pan with two sheets of aluminum foil. Place the springform pan inside a large baking pan.

2. In a large mixing bowl, beat together the eggs and sugar for 3 to 5 minutes, or until they double in volume.

3. In a microwave-safe bowl, combine the chocolate chips and butter. Microwave on high in 30-second intervals until the mixture is melted.

4. Fold the melted chocolate mixture into the egg mixture.

5. Stir in the vanilla extract and salt, then gradually whisk in the cocoa powder. Do not overmix, though; you want to keep the volume.

6. Pour the batter into the prepared springform pan. Carefully pour boiling water into the large baking pan until it comes halfway up the sides of the springform pan.

7. Bake for 35 to 40 minutes, or until the cake is firm in the middle. Allow the cake to cool to room temperature before removing the springform pan sides.

DAIRY-FREE TIP: Replace the butter with a nondairy substitute.

INGREDIENT TIP: Although you're baking, stick to cooking spray instead of baking spray. Baking spray usually contains gluten.

Per serving Calories 514; Fat 39g; Total Carbohydrates 38g; Fiber 1g; Sodium 508mg; Protein 9g

LEMON JELLY BRUNCH CAKE

My husband grew up eating lemon jelly cake as birthday cake. While I personally go for something a little more traditional for my birthday, I think this gluten-free version is absolutely perfect for a brunch get-together. As you can see, it's versatile, so serve it on the special or not-so-special occasion of your choice!

SERVES 8 / PREP TIME: 10 MINUTES / COOK TIME: 25 MINUTES

NUT-FREE

VEGETARIAN

Nonstick cooking spray

1⅓ cups gluten-free baking flour blend

1 teaspoon baking powder

½ teaspoon baking soda

¼ teaspoon salt

⅓ cup granulated sugar

¼ cup brown sugar

3 tablespoons unsalted butter

¼ cup freshly squeezed lemon juice

2 tablespoons grated lemon zest

1 teaspoon vanilla extract

2 large eggs, at room temperature

½ cup whole milk

1 cup confectioners' sugar

3 tablespoons water

1 cup strawberry jelly or jam

1. Preheat the oven to 350°F. Lightly coat two 8-inch cake pans with cooking spray.

2. In a large bowl, whisk together the flour blend, baking powder, baking soda, and salt.

3. In another bowl, cream together the sugars, butter, lemon juice, lemon zest, and vanilla extract. Beat in the eggs.

4. Slowly mix the flour mixture into the butter mixture. Add the milk and whisk until fully combined. Divide the batter evenly between the cake pans. Bake for 20 to 25 minutes, or until an inserted toothpick comes out clean.

5. Allow the cakes to cool in the pans for 10 minutes before transferring them to a wire rack to cool completely.

6. In a small bowl, whisk together the confectioners' sugar and water.

7. Place the first cake layer on a serving plate and spread the jelly over the top, then place the remaining cake layer on top. Drizzle the sugar glaze over the cake and serve.

DAIRY-FREE TIP: Replace the milk and butter with nondairy alternatives.

Per serving Calories 303; Fat 7g; Total Carbohydrates 59g; Fiber 2g; Sodium 211mg; Protein 4g

THE BEST PEANUT BUTTER COOKIES

One day, I decided I just had to have the peanut butter cookies I grew up on, perfectly chewy and packed with nutty flavor. It turns out they taste just as good without gluten. You're welcome!

MAKES 24 COOKIES / PREP TIME: 10 MINUTES / COOK TIME: 10 MINUTES

30-MINUTES

NUT-FREE

VEGETARIAN

1 cup peanut butter

1 large egg

½ cup granulated sugar

½ cup (packed) brown sugar

4 tablespoons (½ stick) unsalted butter, at room temperature

1 cup all-purpose gluten-free flour blend

1 teaspoon baking powder

1 teaspoon baking soda

½ teaspoon salt

1. Preheat the oven to 350°F. Line two rimmed sheet pans with parchment paper.

2. In a large mixing bowl, beat together the peanut butter, egg, sugars, and butter.

3. In another bowl, whisk together the flour blend, baking powder, baking soda, and salt.

4. Sift the flour mixture into the butter mixture and mix until combined.

5. Drop spoonfuls of the dough onto the prepared sheet pans. Use a fork to create a crisscross pattern on the top of each cookie.

6. Bake for 9 to 11 minutes, or until the edges of the cookies turn brown.

7. Allow the cookies to cool on the sheet pans for 5 minutes before transferring them to a wire rack to cool completely.

DAIRY-FREE TIP: Replace the butter with a nondairy alternative.

(1 cookie) Calories 128; Fat 8g; Total Carbohydrates 13g; Fiber 1g; Sodium 169mg; Protein 4g

GRANDMA'S CUTOUT SUGAR COOKIES

In my family, it's a tradition to make our grandma's famous cutout sugar cookies at least once a year. After my diagnosis, I had to make a couple of changes to the recipe to give myself the chance to eat them again. They take a bit of work, but they're totally worth it. They also freeze really well, so you can keep a batch in reserve to heat up whenever you want to serve warm homemade cookies to guests.

MAKES 24 COOKIES / PREP TIME: 10 MINUTES, PLUS 1 HOUR TO CHILL / COOK TIME: 10 MINUTES

NUT-FREE

VEGETARIAN

1 cup (2 sticks) unsalted butter, at room temperature

¾ cups sugar

2 large eggs

¼ cup sour cream

1 teaspoon vanilla extract

2 ¾ cups gluten-free baking flour blend

2 teaspoons ground nutmeg

½ teaspoon baking powder

½ teaspoon salt

1. In a large bowl, cream together the butter and sugar until smooth.

2. Beat in the eggs, sour cream, and vanilla extract.

3. In a small bowl, whisk together the flour blend, nutmeg, baking powder, and salt.

4. Stir the flour mixture into the butter mixture.

5. Wrap the dough in plastic wrap and chill it in the refrigerator for at least 1 hour.

6. Preheat the oven to 350°F.

7. Roll out the dough on a well-floured surface until it's about ¼ inch thick. Use your favorite cookie cutters to cut out cookies in any shape you want.

8. Place the cookies ½ inch apart on two ungreased rimmed sheet pans.

9. Bake for 8 to 10 minutes, or until the edges of the cookies turn brown.

10. Allow the cookies to cool completely before decorating.

DAIRY-FREE TIP: Replace the butter and sour cream with nondairy substitutes.

VEGAN TIP: Swap the eggs out for a vegan egg-replacement option.

(1 cookie) Calories 152; Fat 9g; Total Carbohydrates 17g; Fiber 1g; Sodium 112mg; Protein 2g

QUICK CHOCOLATE PUDDING

Here's a quick treat you can serve in a pinch. Ditch those questionable pudding packets and make your own at home in no time. But be warned: It's so tasty and so easy to make that if you're like me, you might find yourself making it all the time—even late at night!

SERVES 4 / PREP TIME: 5 MINUTES, PLUS 1 HOUR TO CHILL / COOK TIME: 15 MINUTES

NUT-FREE

VEGETARIAN

2 cups whole milk, plus ¼ cup, divided

1 teaspoon unsweetened cocoa powder

¼ teaspoon vanilla extract

¼ teaspoon salt

¼ cup gluten-free cornstarch

1 cup chocolate chips

1. Pour 2 cups of milk into a small saucepan and warm over medium-low heat. Whisk in the cocoa powder, vanilla extract, and salt.

2. In a small bowl, whisk together the cornstarch and remaining ¼ cup of milk.

3. Slowly whisk the cornstarch mixture into the saucepan.

4. Fold in the chocolate chips and stir until melted.

5. Pour the hot pudding into small serving bowls and chill for 1 to 2 hours before serving.

DAIRY-FREE TIP: Replace the milk with a nondairy alternative.

INGREDIENT TIP: Although cornstarch is naturally gluten-free, it's sometimes processed in plants where it can be cross-contaminated. Check the label to be sure.

Per serving Calories 376; Fat 20g; Total Carbohydrates 48g; Fiber 3g; Sodium 191mg; Protein 4g

ONE-MINUTE FRESH WHIPPED CREAM

After finding out how easy it is to make fresh whipped cream, I've never gone back! You won't want to either, because, oh my word, it tastes amazing and gives those questionable store-bought containers a true run for their money. Just a couple of minutes is all you need, and then you'll have fresh whipped cream to put on anything and everything!

SERVES 4 / PREP TIME: 1 MINUTE

5-INGREDIENTS   30-MINUTES

NUT-FREE

VEGETARIAN

2 cups heavy whipping cream, chilled

½ cup confectioners' sugar

1. In a cold medium bowl, beat the heavy cream and confectioners' sugar to stiff peaks.

2. Store in the refrigerator for up to 4 days.

SERVING TIP: Serve on top of Quick Chocolate Pudding (page 120) or Flourless Double-Chocolate Cake (page 114).

Per serving Calories 222; Fat 22g; Total Carbohydrates 5g; Fiber 0g; Sodium 23mg; Protein 1g

Homemade Ranch Dressing (page 129)

CHAPTER NINE

Sauces, Dressings, and Staples

LOW-CARB PIZZA CRUST

I pulled this recipe together one day when I was fed up with cauliflower-based pizza crusts that cooked just fine but fell apart when you actually tried to pick up and eat a slice of pizza. This cheese-based alternative is a fabulous gluten-free, low-carb option with zero yeast needed.

SERVES 4 / PREP TIME: 10 MINUTES / COOK TIME: 30 MINUTES

5-INGREDIENTS

NUT-FREE

VEGETARIAN

1½ cups grated Parmesan cheese

½ cup shredded Monterey Jack cheese

4 ounces cream cheese, at room temperature

2 large eggs, lightly beaten

1 tablespoon gluten-free Italian seasoning

Pizza toppings of choice

1. Preheat the oven to 350°F. Line a rimmed sheet pan with parchment paper.

2. In a medium bowl, combine the Parmesan, Monterey Jack, cream cheese, eggs, and Italian seasoning. Mix until you have a cheese ball–like texture.

3. Spoon the mixture onto the prepared sheet pan and spread it into a rectangle or circle. Smooth out the edges with a spatula to create a crust with more defined edges.

4. Bake for 20 to 25 minutes, or until the crust lightly browns.

5. Remove the crust from the pan by lifting up the parchment paper. Then lay a fresh piece of parchment paper on the sheet pan and carefully flip the pizza crust upside down onto the fresh parchment.

6. Cover the crust with your favorite pizza toppings, then bake for another 10 minutes, or until the toppings are heated and the cheese is melted.

Per serving Calories 324; Fat 23g; Total Carbohydrates 3g; Fiber 0g; Sodium 589mg; Protein 22g

FOUR-INGREDIENT BUFFALO SAUCE

This Buffalo sauce holds a place of honor in our family. It's the sauce that is totally acceptable to put on anything. Simply mix everything in a jar, shake it up, and pour it onto your next delicious meal. Winner.

MAKES 1½ CUPS / PREP TIME: 5 MINUTES

5-INGREDIENTS   30-MINUTES

DAIRY-FREE

NUT-FREE

VEGAN

1 cup gluten-free hot pepper sauce

½ cup gluten-free distilled white vinegar

1½ tablespoons paprika

½ tablespoon garlic powder

1. In a small jar, combine the hot sauce, vinegar, paprika, and garlic powder. Cover the jar and shake well.

2. Store in an airtight container in the refrigerator for up to 3 weeks, shaking the bottle to mix the ingredients well before using.

SERVING TIP: Buffalo sauce can go on so much more than chicken wings! Try it on baked potatoes or Spicy Black Bean Burgers (page 55), or use it as pizza sauce on Low-Carb Pizza Crust (page 124).

INGREDIENT TIP: Because it's distilled, white vinegar should be gluten-free, even if it's made from gluten-containing grains. However, some people do report reacting badly to it, possibly because of cross-contamination at some point during production. To be safe, make sure to buy vinegar made from corn or potatoes rather than wheat, barley, or rye.

(2 tablespoons) Calories 12; Fat 0g; Total Carbohydrates 2g; Fiber 1g; Sodium 2mg; Protein 1g

HOMEMADE TACO SEASONING

I kid you not, once you start making taco seasoning at home, you'll never go back to buying those seasoning packets at the grocery store. It's so simple to make yourself, not to mention much more cost-effective, that it's just crazy not to do it. Plus you can be absolutely sure there's no gluten.

MAKES ABOUT 2 TABLESPOONS / PREP TIME: 10 MINUTES / COOK TIME: 12 MINUTES

30-MINUTES

DAIRY-FREE

NUT-FREE

VEGAN

1 tablespoon chili powder

1½ teaspoons ground cumin

1 teaspoon garlic powder

1 teaspoon onion powder

¼ teaspoon salt

¼ teaspoon red pepper flakes

¼ teaspoon cayenne pepper

1. In a small jar, combine the chili powder, cumin, garlic powder, onion powder, salt, red pepper flakes, and cayenne powder. Cover the jar and shake a couple of times to mix the spices.

2. To use, add the contents of the jar and ¼ cup water to 1 pound cooked ground meat.

(1 teaspoon) Calories 14; Fat 1g; Total Carbohydrates 2g; Fiber 1g; Sodium 113mg; Protein 1g

BEST TACO SAUCE EVER

I named this recipe "Best Taco Sauce Ever" for a reason. If I were allowed to have only one sauce for the rest of my life, I would choose this one. I couldn't survive without taco salads, and this sauce can transform any taco salad from good to mind-blowing.

MAKES ABOUT 2 CUPS / PREP TIME: 5 MINUTES

30-MINUTES

DAIRY-FREE

NUT-FREE

VEGETARIAN

1 (15-ounce) can gluten-free tomato sauce

⅓ cup water

2 tablespoons gluten-free distilled white vinegar

1½ teaspoons ground cumin

1 teaspoon honey

1 teaspoon garlic powder

1 teaspoon onion powder

½ teaspoon paprika

½ teaspoon chili powder

¼ teaspoon cayenne pepper

1. In a medium bowl, whisk together the tomato sauce, water, vinegar, cumin, honey, garlic powder, onion powder, paprika, chili powder, and cayenne pepper until combined.

2. If the sauce is a little too thick, add water, 1 tablespoon at a time, until it reaches your desired thickness.

3. Store in an airtight container for up to 3 weeks.

INGREDIENT TIP: Store-bought sauces can contain gluten. Check the label on your tomato sauce to be sure it's gluten-free. Because it's distilled, white vinegar should be gluten-free even if it's produced from gluten-containing grains. To be extra safe, buy vinegar made from corn or potatoes rather than wheat, barley, or rye.

(¼ cup) Calories 25; Fat 1g; Total Carbohydrates 5g; Fiber 1g; Sodium 283mg; Protein 1g

HOMEMADE RANCH SEASONING

As delicious as store-bought ranch seasoning mixes can be, anything in a packet is at least a little bit questionable. It's so much easier, cheaper, and, frankly, tastier to make this mixture at home with simple spices and be free from any worry about what's actually in those packets!

MAKES ABOUT ⅓ CUP / PREP TIME: 5 MINUTES

30-MINUTES

DAIRY-FREE

NUT-FREE

VEGAN

2 tablespoons dried parsley

1 tablespoon dried chives

2 teaspoons garlic powder

2 teaspoons onion powder

2 teaspoons dried
  onion flakes

1 teaspoon dried dill weed

1 teaspoon salt

1 teaspoon freshly ground
  black pepper

In a small jar, combine the parsley, chives, garlic powder, onion powder, onion flakes, dill weed, salt, and pepper. Close the jar and shake a couple of times to mix the spices.

(1 tablespoon) Calories 10; Fat 0g; Total Carbohydrates 2g; Fiber 0g; Sodium 390mg; Protein 0g

HOMEMADE RANCH DRESSING

When I was growing up, my mother always made our ranch dressing with store-bought ranch seasoning packets. It was a good way to avoid some of the additives in store-bought ranch dressing. Once I discovered the wonder of making my own seasoning packets, I realized I could start making my own ranch dressing from scratch! You won't believe how amazing something can taste with just three simple ingredients.

MAKES 1 CUP / PREP TIME: 5 MINUTES, PLUS AT LEAST 1 HOUR TO CHILL

5-INGREDIENTS

NUT-FREE

VEGETARIAN

½ cup Homemade Mayonnaise (page 131)

½ cup whole milk

3 tablespoons Homemade Ranch Seasoning (page 128)

1. Combine the mayonnaise, milk, and ranch seasoning in a jar with a tight lid. Shake for 30 to 45 seconds.

2. Chill in the refrigerator for at least 1 hour, or ideally 24 hours, before using.

INGREDIENT TIP: Store-bought condiments can contain gluten. If you use store-bought mayonnaise, check the label to make sure it's gluten-free. Because it's distilled, white vinegar should be gluten-free, even if it's produced from gluten-containing grains. But to be extra safe, buy vinegar made from corn or potatoes rather than wheat, barley, or rye.

(2 tablespoons) Calories 72; Fat 5g; Total Carbohydrates 4g; Fiber 0g; Sodium 257mg; Protein 1g

HOMEMADE BARBECUE SAUCE

Ditch the bottled stuff with its questionable ingredients and make this home-made barbecue sauce instead! It'll be a mega hit at your next summer cookout.

MAKES ABOUT 2 CUPS / PREP TIME: 5 MINUTES / COOK TIME: 15 MINUTES

30-MINUTES

DAIRY-FREE

NUT-FREE

VEGETARIAN

½ teaspoon olive oil

2½ teaspoons minced garlic

1 (6-ounce) can gluten-free tomato paste

¼ cup gluten-free distilled white vinegar

¼ cup gluten-free Worcestershire sauce

¼ cup honey

2 tablespoons gluten-free honey mustard

1½ tablespoons onion powder

1 tablespoon chili powder

1 tablespoon smoked paprika

½ tablespoon salt

1. In a small saucepan, heat the olive oil over low heat. Add the garlic and sauté for 1 minute.

2. Add the tomato paste, vinegar, Worcestershire sauce, honey, honey mustard, onion powder, chili powder, paprika, and salt. Stir until fully combined.

3. Turn the heat down to a simmer and cook for 12 minutes, stirring occasionally.

4. Remove the saucepan from the heat and allow the sauce to cool.

5. Transfer the sauce to an airtight container. Store in the refrigerator for up to 3 weeks.

INGREDIENT TIP: Store-bought condiments can contain gluten. Check the labels on your vinegar, Worcestershire sauce, tomato paste, and mustard to make sure they're gluten-free. Because it's distilled, white vinegar should be gluten-free even if it's produced from gluten-containing grains. To be extra safe, buy vinegar made from corn or potatoes rather than wheat, barley, or rye.

(2 tablespoons) Calories 48; Fat 0g; Total Carbohydrates 11g; Fiber 1g; Sodium 285mg; Protein 1g

HOMEMADE MAYONNAISE

When you run out of mayonnaise and need some in a pinch, you can turn to this recipe. It's also great if you want or need to avoid certain oils! Store-bought mayonnaise often contains soybean oil, for example. I love using a very light olive oil. Put it on your burgers, sandwiches, and wraps, or use it to whip up some Homemade Ranch Dressing (page 129).

MAKES ABOUT 1 CUP / PREP TIME: 5 MINUTES

5-INGREDIENTS　　**30-MINUTES**

DAIRY-FREE

NUT-FREE

VEGETARIAN

1 large egg yolk, at room temperature

2 tablespoons freshly squeezed lemon juice, at room temperature

1 tablespoon gluten-free honey mustard

½ teaspoon salt

¾ cup light olive oil

1. In a food processor or blender, blend the egg yolk, lemon juice, honey mustard, and salt for 10 to 15 seconds.

2. Keeping the blender running, slowly pour in the olive oil in a steady stream. After 2 to 4 minutes, you'll begin to see the mixture thicken and turn creamy.

3. Store in an airtight container in the refrigerator for up to 2 weeks.

INGREDIENT TIP: Store-bought condiments can contain gluten. Check the label on your mustard to make sure it's gluten-free.

(1 tablespoon) Calories 87; Fat 10g; Total Carbohydrates 1g; Fiber 0g; Sodium 79mg; Protein 0g

QUICK PICKLED ONIONS

The pickling process can take a long time, but these pickled onions are ready to eat in under half an hour, with only 5 minutes of work! You've got to try them if you haven't had them before. They enhance everything from burgers to tacos to salads.

MAKES ABOUT 2 CUPS / PREP TIME: 5 MINUTES, PLUS 20 MINUTES TO CHILL

5-INGREDIENTS   **30-MINUTES**

DAIRY-FREE

NUT-FREE

VEGAN

1 medium red onion, roughly chopped

1 to 2 cups apple cider vinegar

1. Put the chopped onions in a glass jar and pour the vinegar over them until they're covered.

2. Seal the jar and chill in the fridge for at least 20 minutes before serving.

3. Use within the week.

(¼ cup) Calories 18; Fat 0g; Total Carbohydrates 2g; Fiber 0g; Sodium 4mg; Protein 0g

TWO-INGREDIENT VANILLA EXTRACT

A bottle of homemade vanilla extract is a fabulous gift idea for anyone, gluten-free or not—just remember to keep one or two for yourself! All you need is two ingredients, and you'll have a vanilla extract that really makes all your baked goods taste great. I like to use 4-ounce bottles and make 16 of them, but you can always use bigger bottles and make fewer.

MAKES 16 (4-OUNCE) BOTTLES / PREP TIME: 10 MINUTES

5-INGREDIENTS   30-MINUTES

DAIRY-FREE

NUT-FREE

VEGAN

25 fresh vanilla beans

½ gallon vodka

1. Cut the vanilla beans into pieces that fit inside 16 (4-ounce) bottles.

2. Slice the vanilla beans down the middle to expose the "caviar," and put 2 or 3 beans in each bottle.

3. Using a funnel, pour ½ cup vodka into each bottle. Seal with a lid.

4. Store the bottles in your pantry for at least 2 months before using.

INGREDIENT TIP: As a distilled alcohol, vodka is naturally gluten-free, no matter what grains It's distilled from. However, some people do report having reactions to vodka made of gluten-containing grains, possibly because of cross-contamination at some point during production. To be safe, use an explicitly gluten-free vodka distilled from potatoes, corn, or grapes; many mainstream brands qualify.

(1 teaspoon) Calories 11; Fat 0g; Total Carbohydrates 0g; Fiber 0g; Sodium 0mg; Protein 0g

The Dirty Dozen and the Clean Fifteen

A nonprofit and environmental watchdog organization called the Environmental Working Group (EWG) looks at data supplied by the US Department of Agriculture (USDA) and the Food and Drug Administration (FDA) about pesticide residues. Each year, it compiles a list of the lowest and highest pesticide loads found in commercial crops. You can use these lists to decide which fruits and vegetables to buy organic to minimize your exposure to pesticides and which conventional produce is considered safe enough to eat. This does not mean they are pesticide free, though, so wash these (and all) fruits and vegetables thoroughly.

These lists change every year, so make sure you look up the most recent one before you fill your shopping cart. You'll find the most recent lists as well as a guide to pesticides in produce at EWG.org/FoodNews.

THE DIRTY DOZEN

Apples • Celery • Cherry tomatoes • Cucumbers • Grapes
Nectarines (imported) • Peaches • Potatoes • Snap peas (imported)
Spinach • Strawberries • Sweet bell peppers
(Kale/Collard greens • Hot peppers)**

** In addition to the dirty dozen, the EWG added two produce items contaminated with highly toxic organophosphate insecticides.

THE CLEAN FIFTEEN

Asparagus • Avocados • Cabbage • Cantaloupes (domestic) • Cauliflower
Eggplant • Grapefruit • Kiwifruit • Mangos • Onions • Papayas • Pineapples
Sweet corn • Sweet peas (frozen) • Sweet potatoes

Measurements and Conversions

VOLUME EQUIVALENTS (LIQUID)

US STANDARD	US STANDARD (OUNCES)	METRIC (APPROXIMATE)
2 tablespoons	1 fl. oz.	30 mL
¼ cup	2 fl. oz.	60 mL
½ cup	4 fl. oz.	120 mL
1 cup	8 fl. oz.	240 mL
1½ cups	12 fl. oz.	355 mL
2 cups or 1 pint	16 fl. oz.	475 mL
4 cups or 1 quart	32 fl. oz.	1 L
1 gallon	128 fl. oz.	4 L

OVEN TEMPERATURES

FAHRENHEIT (F)	CELSIUS (C) (APPROXIMATE)
250°F	120°C
300°F	150°C
325°F	165°C
350°F	180°C
375°F	190°C
400°F	200°C
425°F	220°C
450°F	230°C

VOLUME EQUIVALENTS (DRY)

US STANDARD	METRIC (APPROXIMATE)
⅛ teaspoon	0.5 mL
¼ teaspoon	1 mL
½ teaspoon	2 mL
¾ teaspoon	4 mL
1 teaspoon	5 mL
1 tablespoon	15 mL
¼ cup	59 mL
⅓ cup	79 mL
½ cup	118 mL
⅔ cup	156 mL
¾ cup	177 mL
1 cup	235 mL
2 cups or 1 pint	475 mL
3 cups	700 mL
4 cups or 1 quart	1 L
½ gallon	2 L
1 gallon	4 L

WEIGHT EQUIVALENTS

US STANDARD	METRIC (APPROXIMATE)
½ ounce	15 g
1 ounce	30 g
2 ounces	60 g
4 ounces	115 g
8 ounces	225 g
12 ounces	340 g
16 ounces or 1 pound	455 g

Resources

Bob's Red Mill (www.bobsredmill.com): A company that makes natural, organic grain products and baking supplies, including many outstanding gluten-free options. Their Gluten-Free 1-to-1 Baking Flour is my absolute favorite!

Celiac Disease Foundation (www.celiac.org): A great resource and nonprofit organization that raises awareness about celiac disease and advocates for people affected by it.

Gluten-Free Certification Organization (www.gfco.org): Provides certification services and information on gluten-free products.

Glutino (www.glutino.com): A company that makes fabulous gluten-free snacks, baked goods, and baking supplies.

Jovial (www.jovialfoods.com): My favorite gluten-free pasta brand, with all sorts of fantastic shapes and sizes of pasta I've never been able to find anywhere else.

Meaningful Eats (www.meaningfuleats.com): Another great gluten-free blog with plenty of excellent recipes.

VeggieBalance (www.veggiebalance.com): My gluten-free blog, which offers over 300 recipes that make baking, cooking, and eating easy every day.

Recipe Label Index

Recipe Index

Index

About the Author

Lindsay Garza is a gluten-free blogger at VeggieBalance.com and author of *The Gluten-Free Party Food Cookbook*. When she's not in the kitchen, she is traveling the world, learning the ins and outs of traveling while gluten-free so she can share them with her readers. She and her husband live in Michigan with their dog and cat.

CPSIA information can be obtained
at www.ICGtesting.com
Printed in the USA
LVHW011950141218
600510LV00005B/5